90-Day Profit Reset

Gain Your Independence from Reduced Cash Flow, Evaporating Customers, and Shrinking Margins

By Wayne J. Belisle, CPA

90-Day Profit Reset
Gain Your Independence from Reduced Cash Flow, Evaporating Customers, and Shrinking Margins

Published by Profit Maximizer Publishing
11208 Montwood
El Paso, Tx. 79936

ISBN: 978-1-7355098-0-8

Cover design by Jim Saurbaugh | JS Graphic Design

DISCLAIMER AND/OR LEGAL NOTICES

While the publisher and author have used their best efforts in preparing this book, they make no representations or warranties with respect to the accuracy or completeness of the contents of this book. The advice and strategies contained herein may not be suitable for your situation. You should consult a professional where appropriate. Neither the publisher nor the author shall be liable for any loss of profit or any other commercial damages, including but not limited to special, incidental, consequential, or other damages. The purchaser or reader of this publication assumes responsibility for the use of these materials and information. Adherence to all applicable laws and regulations, both advertising and all other aspects of doing business in the United States or any other jurisdiction, is the sole responsibility of the purchaser or reader.

This book is intended to provide accurate information with regard to the subject matter covered. However, the Author and the Publisher accept no responsibility for inaccuracies or omissions, and the

Dedicated to my wife, Dora, and my incredible children, Jessica, Eric and Vanessa who have been with me on this crazy entrepreneurial roller coaster ride. Love you all now and forever!

Table of Contents

Foreword

Ask business owners who they trust with the most intimate details of their business and they'll usually respond, in this order: their accountant, their attorney, and perhaps their insurance agent.

I've often referred to my CPA as the person I trust most to stay current on tax law, so I stay lean, mean, and legal while I build my business. What I've learned from working with Wayne Belisle is that while he is an extraordinary CPA, he is so much more than simply a "numbers" person.

In addition to being a highly skilled CPA and trusted tax advisor with 40 years of experience, Wayne is also one of the savviest marketers I know. As a marketer and business coach to small business owners, early on in our relationship, I would often marvel at the marketing and business-building wisdom Wayne would share.

On one of our calls, after Wayne shared some "pearl of wisdom," I remember asking him, in a somewhat off-handed manner, "Wayne, how did a numbers guy like you get so smart about marketing and business-growth strategies?" His answer stuck with me all these years.

He said, "Well Jim, when you work with hundreds of business owners in multiple industries for 40 years, and you keep your eyes open, you learn a thing or two. You not only get to see what works from the inside, on the balance sheet, you also learn a great deal about what marketing and growth plans are working."

My reply may have caught Wayne off guard. I said, "Wayne, you may not see this, but you're one helluva business coach, and you should write a book!" After a few months of prodding, you're holding that book!

The *90-Day Profit Reset* is more than a simple book with a big promise. It was written for a specific reason, and for many businesses that have experienced a setback, it is exactly what is needed at this exact moment in history.

This book will provide you with three highly important and actionable strategies that you can take right now to improve the financial health of your business... in 90 days!

The three strategies – your game plan for the next 90 days – are:

1. Reinvigorate Your Cash Flow
2. Re-Engage Your Customers
3. Supercharge Your Profit Margins

As Wayne so eloquently writes in this book, "Successful business owners know that the secret to massively increasing profits is the combination of good ideas coupled with a laser focus on regular action." Wayne's mantra is: ***Good ideas plus action equals massive profits.***

In keeping with the spirit of this mantra, my advice to you is: read this book now (get some good ideas), then immediately put them into action, with laser focus, and you'll be amazed at the results (massive profits).

Jim Palmer
The Dream Business Coach
www.getjimpalmer.com

Introduction
Business as Usual... Or Not!

The "new economy" has created a new business rule: Keep doing what you're doing... and you will go broke.

This rule first reared its head after the 2008 banking collapse that tightened credit and drove many businesses out of business. Then came the explosive changes to the way we run our businesses due to the wild popularity of social media followed quickly by the advent and growth of smartphone apps and online business competition.

And then came the terrible effects of the pandemic of 2020 that brought with it disruptions resulting from stay-at-home mandates and businesses forced to close.

I'm Wayne Belisle, and I'm a CPA who's been working with business owners since I was a sophomore in college... way back in 1975. I'm the founder and owner of a local CPA firm started in 1991. We help small business owners file their taxes correctly; pay as little in taxes as legally possible (yes, I like my clients, but I'm not sharing a jail cell with them), saving them five million dollars over the last four years; and finally, help clients massively increase their profits.

That last part – massively increase their profits – is what sets me apart. I'm not just another CPA who will give tax advice. I want to help my clients truly grow their businesses and their bottom lines. I have the experience and business sense to help them do that, and it's exactly why I wrote this book.

My goal of helping business owners massively increase profits is why I first started my award-winning blog,

"Small Business Profit Maximizer: Ideas You Can Use to Make This Your Most Profitable Year Ever" about ten years ago. I also launched a private Facebook group, The Profit-Maximizing Club where I share relevant videos three to five times each week, and I also created Wayne Belisle's Profit Master Academy where I share profit-maximizing courses, including two free ones. (You can find the links at the back in the Resource section.)

I know there is so much more to running a profitable business than filing your taxes correctly, and with my knowledge and experience, I've become so much more than "just a CPA" for my clients. In this book, I am going to share my answers to the many business owners who've reached out to me saying, "I need help. My business isn't paying the bills. I'm worried that I'll have to go back to work for someone else."

Whether or not you share that fear or simply want to see more money on your bottom line and in your bank account, I've written this book for you.

Taking Action vs. Making Excuses

Let's jump right in with the approach I take with my clients. The first thing I emphasize is that they have to accept reality. To succeed as an entrepreneur you have to replace excuses with action. I see many business owners who barely make enough to pay bills and survive… with little if any left for anything else, like growth or enjoying some time off. I've been there too. Many are struggling with not making enough to take care of their families – *working harder than ever and actually making less money*.

There are millions of excuses any business owner can give for the inability to change their current situation. But these excuses only sabotage success. I've heard 'em all: "The economy isn't good right now; I can't compete with the big guys; banks won't lend me money; I can't afford to spend money on marketing..." and on and on.

Excuses are caused by our own fears. They're created in our minds as a way to avoid and ignore our innermost doubts. Excuses lead to two things: inaction and zero results.

If you are unhappy with your current situation, you and only you can change it... and you must. If there's something you don't like about your current business, you created it, so change it. You're the "god" of your business; you created it out of nothing and now it exists as a viable business or one that could be not only viable but extremely profitable if you made a few changes.

> *Excuses are only good for generating inaction and zero results.*

It's time to change your mindset. Think about the worst-case scenario you envision for your business. You may not have to think very hard as we are still in the shadow of COVID-19 as I write this. In talking with clients, I'm hearing a lot of concerns about their businesses. "What if I can't reopen the business after the pandemic?" Sure, it's a big concern, but my reply is: "Okay, what if you can't? What *would* you do if you couldn't reopen your business?"

If you can't live with that scenario, there's no point in thinking, "I should have done x, y, or z" or "One day, I'll do this" as your answer. Right now is the time to create a plan to strengthen your business. If you don't want to return to the workforce employed by someone else or if you can't live with your current situation, you need to change it.

It's really that simple. And now you should be grasping that what you will read in this book really has nothing to do with filing taxes and everything to do with re-setting your profitability in 90 days or fewer.

I understand that you have doubts and fears as an entrepreneur. We all do, my clients and myself included. So make a list of those fears, then go down that list and figure out how you eliminate or mitigate each one. Then create a plan for your business goals that includes a monthly action to achieve those goals. Once you put your plan into action every month, you'll prevent new excuses from forming in your mind.

The important thing to understand is that ***now is the time to act if you want to change your future.*** There is never a better time to start. I actually love recessions. That really sounds harsh and even a little crazy, but read on to see why. Yes, recessions throw some people out of business and that's very sad, but for those who survive, it's a fantastic time to attack and grow the business. Why? Right now, prices are lower. Suppliers are hurting too and much more likely to strike deals and work with you on costs in order to make a sale. Take advantage of this opportunity!

With more businesses closing, there is less competition during a recession. It gives you the opportunity to increase your profits dramatically as the economy rebounds.

Technology makes it easier for small business owners to compete with the big companies. Anyone can take their business online and use social media, webinars, eBooks, digital magazines, etc. for promotion. The options are endless. Moreover, because of the pandemic, customers and suppliers are now far more accustomed to doing business online and working remotely. The remote work opportunity also eliminates geographic boundaries. If you are looking for talent, you can find people anywhere. Add high unemployment to the mix, with people looking for work, and the pool from which you can hire is much larger. Yes, it's sad, but when businesses closed during the pandemic, there became an abundance of great employees – employees who are now much more willing to work for a smart small business owner than a large conglomerate. Events over the last decade (not just during the pandemic) revealed the idea of job security being greater with a large company than a small one as an illusion.

I just pointed out the silver linings that exist, so remember that excuses are obstacles to your success. When you allow them to exist, you are sabotaging your business and future profits. Replace excuses with a monthly plan of action steps. Follow the plan. Achieve the goals. Then watch your business flourish and add to your pocketbook.

What About Right Now?

Perhaps you're like some of my clients who ask, "Yeah, but my business is in trouble now. What do I do *right now*?"

During the Great 2008 Recession over ten years ago and as I write this during the 2020 pandemic, I heard this question a lot. Honestly, the one mistake that most small business owners make is to wait too long to decide (or admit) they have a problem. This only further complicates the recovery because the longer you wait to move into survival mode, the more likely it is that you'll need to take very drastic measures.

The biggest mistake I saw during the COVID-19 quarantine and shut down was business owners failing to take it seriously from the very beginning. The second biggest mistake I saw was the reaction: "Wow, I got this loan from the government, so it solves all my problems." Sorry, but it doesn't.

Business as usual is going to change and, in some instances, has already changed. Many customers may be scared to physically come back into your business, perhaps by the contagious nature of the virus or scared to spend money because they've been laid off or have taken some other financial hit, perhaps still being behind on their bills. If they had to dip into their emergency savings, they are now faced with shoring that up again. If they never had an emergency savings, they learned a hard lesson about its importance and are now saving. Regardless, your consumer has changed the way they think and spend. We definitely saw that reaction in 2008, and as I write this, I'm sure we are going to see a repeat.

So what about now? What do you do now?

First, start with accurate accounting records that will provide you with the reports you'll need to review constantly in order to identify the early warning signs of trouble. When is it time to go into survival mode? For most, it's obvious:

when they can't collect enough revenue to pay mounting bills. But I don't want you to wait that long.

Here are some early warning signs about looming trouble before you actually run out of cash:

> *Accurate record keeping provides the early warning signs of trouble ahead.*

- More cash going out weekly than coming in. If you don't have good accounting records, how will you know?
- Your bank account balance falls below your normal cash balance for two straight months. You should have a sense of your normal balance, and if you see it start to drop, don't wait.
- Future sales projections have reduced dramatically. What's that? You're not projecting sales? We're going to cover that, and you need to do it, so you have some insight and foresight about brewing trouble.
- Not paying your 941 payroll tax deposits on time is a big, red flag. Failing to pay these on time is a number one sign that something is wrong with the business. It's a symptom of a problem; it's not the cause of the problem.

Survival Mode

So what's the first thing you should do if you find yourself in survival mode? First, you have to adjust your attitude. Your ability to adapt to your current situation is the number one predictor of whether or not the company is going to survive. Stop panicking. Stop. Take a deep breath. Accept the reality. Start planning.

Second, understand that the current situation – whether it's a current recession or one on the horizon – is real. Failure will severely affect your family, employees, and creditors.

Third, eliminate the blame game and accept responsibility. As the business owner, it's always your fault. You own the business and the buck stops with you.

Fourth, forget the past. Fixating on your mistakes will just enable you to keep making excuses... and I'm guilty of this one as well. Thank goodness my wife and business coach can knock me out of it when it hits.

Next, go into business overdrive. Focus on essential tasks only. Don't answer non-business emails, don't waste time on social media, don't take personal calls, forget golf and vacations for a while. Your job is to save your business.

Yes, it will be hard. I know that. Yes, survival mode will take extra time and energy; however, it is time and energy you must spend.

Moving Forward

That said, I want you to also always visualize success. Put your goals on paper and post them where you see them all the time. They will be a reminder and motivating factor to stay the course.

Now, a business must create a detailed cash budget. For example, you have to know that you'll need $10,000 for Friday's payroll at least a week in advance and not when you sit down to write paychecks. A cash budget is the early warning system that you need to act.

Next, you'll have to cut costs. Literally review every single expense and eliminate those that don't have any effect on your customers' experience or that don't help you to provide a better product. Be honest and brutal. It's sink or swim time. Don't think of it as being cheap. Think of it as being frugal. Think of it as concentrating on survival.

Review your labor costs. Employees are often the largest cost that is under your control. Cut non-essential employees, cut hours, hire temps as needed, initiate temporary unpaid furloughs, and it's time for you to work harder than ever. Get out of your chair and get back into the trenches. Yes, it's tough on everyone, but it is survival mode, and if you don't survive, everyone loses. You can always rehire and adjust salaries once you see your way clear.

Delay purchasing equipment and supplies as long as possible. Use it up and wear it out. Don't carry excess inventory.

Use the barter system. Cash is the lifeblood of your business, so guard it closely. See if you can trade services rather than shelling out cash. Negotiate price reductions at the time of purchase. Just ask, "Is this the best price you can give me?" If they say it is, let them know you will have to get other quotes. This one statement often gets you a better deal.

Ask to renegotiate credit terms with vendors and for long-term financing. Pay with a credit card, and then pay that balance in full before the due date, so you can buy yourself an extra 30 days at no cost. Negotiate a reduction in outstanding invoices with your vendors, ask for price cuts, or long-term funding. Caution: Do not do this with your essential vendors.

Speed up your own cash collections. Failure to collect accounts receivables in a timely manner is the number one reason behind cash flow problems. Make collections your main priority. Call, call, and call again those customers who are in arrears. In a recession, they may be in the same boat, but they'll often pay the squeaky wheel – you.

Ask for deposits at the time of the order and request prepayments. Tighten your own terms and ask for payment in full as soon as the product or service is delivered.

Research and resolve any customer complaints. This is the best way to expedite their payment. If you don't take care of their concerns or questions, they often withhold payment.

Commit time and energy to your sales and marketing program. Sales drive your revenue and your business, so give them a boost! Once you've cut costs and increased collections, increasing revenue is the next step in survival mode. Figure out how to enhance your sales and marketing program and then do it.

> *"Stopping advertising to save money is like stopping your watch to save time."*
>
> *~ Henry Ford*

Increase your profit margin. If the sale is $100 and the product cost (including labor and materials) is currently $50, reducing the product cost to $45 or $40 will greatly increase your bottom line. This one change will make a huge difference in your financial situation.

Finally, look for a source of outside funding until your sales and marketing efforts pay off. For example, cash advances on open lines of credit or credit cards, apply for loans (when you catch the problem early, your financials are usually still strong and the time to get a line of credit is before you actually need it), offer a discount for prepayments, borrow from your or your spouse's 401(k), get a second mortgage, sell off excess business or personal property and equipment, and if you have to, get loans from friends and family.

Remember: It's survival time, so put your pride aside and do what's in your business's and wallet's best interest. I know these suggestions sound and are extreme. You have a responsibility to everyone who relies on your business to make it survive.

Admittedly, I just scratched the surface, but don't worry. The entire next chapter is dedicated to these topics and more in greater detail.

If you are not struggling, and skipped over the last section, go back and read or reread it because all of these things are very helpful to businesses that are not struggling. Obviously, the best thing is to never have to get into a situation in which you are faced with survival mode, and everything I just listed can help keep you out of survival mode.

Applying these steps and the rest of what is to come in the rest of the book will lead you to a highly successful business that you can enjoy and be proud of.

So let's get started!

Chapter One

Reinvigorate Your Cash Flow

Perhaps you've heard, "Cash is king." Cash flow is critical to any and every business, large or small. A cash flow crunch quickly leads to crisis. However, did you know there is actually cash hiding in your business? In the 40-plus years I've been working with business owners, they are always amazed to learn the surprising amount of cash they didn't know they had or were leaving on the table.

In tough times or boom times, tracking every dollar and ensuring your cash is spent wisely always leads to more cash in your bank account. Making changes early can be the important difference between success and bankruptcy.

Let's look at a few ideas that increase cash flow quickly.

First, increase sales. Almost every business ignores the one sales area that is an absolute gold mine: current customers. As a business owner, if you do nothing else that I cover in this book, this is an area on which to focus. Increase your lead conversion, so you're turning more of your contacts into sales. Next, since your existing customers are already buying from you, increase each sales order size by upselling. Take a look at your products and services that logically fit together. Ensure your existing customers know *everything* that you do. ***Don't assume they know it.*** Train your staff to upsell and always offer more. Third, improve your systems to increase repeat sales. This might include incentives for your customers to shop with you more frequently. Increase your communication with your customers about new products and services that solve their problems. Create or improve your system for referrals. Besides an existing customer, a referral is your next easiest sale. Ask your best customers who else might benefit from working with you. (When you're done reading this book, check out *The Referral Engine* by John Jantsch.)

Another quick way to increase sales and cash flow is to increase your prices. It is the quickest, easiest way to increase your revenue. If you're worried about losing customers, there's an equation that I'll cover later that reveals the surprising number of customers you have to lose before you're negatively impacted and really start losing money. ***You'll discover that when you raise prices, you will actually make more money... with less work.***

Speed up your collections. Get in the important habit of reviewing your receivables every single week. Call every customer as soon as they are past due. There's no secret to successful collection. You simply have to stay on top of the past dues. If you feel hesitant to do so, just remember: it's your money.

Another place cash is usually hiding is in inventory. The better you control your inventory, the more money you'll have. Money tied up in inventory is money that could be in your bank account. It's money that can't be put to work for you. Examine your inventory and identify items that are not selling quickly. Lower the price of these items to move them off your shelves. Again, the math proves that it is better to sell today at a ten-percent discount than six months from now at full price. If it doesn't sell at ten-percent off, it's still better to offer 25 percent off than leave it on the shelf for a year. If that doesn't work, actually sell it at cost and reinvest the money in your profitable products. Don't be too proud to admit that a particular product was a mistake. Ultimately, if discounts or selling at cost don't attract buyers, sell it below cost rather than allowing it to become completely obsolete and headed for the trash.

There is an obvious relationship between cash flow and expenses. When you decrease the latter, the former goes up... quickly. However, a ten-percent across-the-board cut probably won't work. For example, cutting advertising has the negative consequence of cutting sales. Instead, review your expenses line by line, looking for items that can be reduced or even eliminated altogether. We all fall into the trap of inertia. If you haven't reviewed your contracts for things like insurance and phone service, you could well be paying too much for it. Time to ask for bids again.

Finally, to quickly increase cash flow, reduce your outgoing cash. Ask customers to supply their own raw materials or explore just-in-time inventory processes. As a last option, look into floor-plan financing of your inventory. Your suppliers also have a stake in your survival and success, so they'll often work with you when you can demonstrate that it's in their best interest. Ask for longer payment terms, even if it means higher prices – but keep a close eye on your margin. Can you pass along the higher price? To reduce outgoing cash flow, always ask yourself, "Can I live without this right now?" If you can, wait and keep that cash in your bank account.

Cutting Expenses

Let's take a closer look at cutting expenses in the 90-day profit reset because that is the quickest way to increase cash. Yes, increasing sales is important in any profit enhancement plan (and I'm going to dedicate the next chapter to it), but cost cutting is the best place to start, so we'll start there.

If your business operates on a ten-percent net profit margin (you have $10 left in the bank for every $100 sale), a $1.00-cost reduction is equivalent to a $10.00 increase in sales. That's important math, and yes, it works exactly like that.

You should do a cost audit annually, or ideally, even more frequently. Identify your biggest costs and assign them to cost centers. A cost center would represent each of the major sections of your business. In a construction business, cost centers might be broken down by commercial and residential. A retail business might have cost centers created by types of customers.

Once you identify your cost centers, use these centers to allocate the remaining costs. When you categorize your costs and understand their relationship to your business, you have a clear picture of where and how to cut costs. Many companies attempt to cost cut and often fail.

Successful cost cutting requires two simple but painful rules:

1. Make it a continuous activity handled by only one or two people. Don't handle it by committee. Too many businesses look to cost cutting only during a business downturn. Win big by having managers look at cost cutting every day. Require quarterly reports about their cost-cutting results. It not only helps during bad times, it substantially boosts your bottom line in boom times. Crash

cost-cutting programs typically result in process hang ups and quality problems because the approach is usually knee-jerk and without a strategic plan. Continuous cost cutting allows you to carefully test results.

2. Cut major costs first. That may seem obvious to you; however, I've been in countless meetings with clients in which they only end up cutting a mere one percent from a very small cost center. Be creative and put on your thinking cap for ways to cut costs that do not hinder efficiency or reduce quality or productivity. I've seen up to 90 percent of costs to be in two areas: cost of goods sold and labor. Yet, these are the toughest places to make cuts. Too often, I've seen business owners focus on a $50/month phone bill reduction rather than spending time working on cuts in these major costs. Eliminate, rather than reduce, certain activities whenever possible.

When looking at a cost center, the first question you should ask is: "Can we get rid of this entirely?" Of course, the answer is almost always "no." Rephrase that question: "Suppose we were *forced* to stop doing this. What would we do instead? How would we get the work done? Would that be cheaper?" Do not even consider your options for reducing the cost of an activity until you have convincing evidence that it's impossible to eliminate it.

Let me share some examples. In my own case, every CPA firm for the last hundred or more years has had a bookkeeping department and have done payroll returns. In

2018, I eliminated all bookkeeping. We outsourced it and stopped doing it. Yes, I got some pushback from clients, but we just don't do it any more. In 2019, we got rid of preparing payroll returns. What happened? First, my income went down – sales down by $40,000. But I'm not in the business to make sales. I'm in the business of increasing my profit. My bottom line increased by $80,000 despite the $40,000 dip in sales. How? First I was able to cut my payroll costs in half and I was no longer wasting time on low-cost and lower profit margin clients. Instead, I spent time on the activities for which clients would pay top dollar.

In another example, one of my clients – a consultant – told me his business was driving him crazy. So he kept his top ten clients and sold the rest of the business. He's now working part time and generating more profits. Not bad.

It's Not a Sale Until…

It's not actually a sale until the money is in the bank. The next quickest way to reinvigorate your cash flow is to create a sound receivables collection system. Having one eliminates most cash problems.

A recent study showed that nearly half of all small businesses are having trouble collecting receivables. Maybe you're nodding your head. During good times, it's an annoyance; however, during bad times, this is often a quick path to an appointment with a bankruptcy attorney.

Collecting receivables requires a plan and a system that addresses collections both *before* and after the sale is complete. Before the sale, you should review the customer's ability to pay. Big companies can use credit reports, but for most small companies, the easiest method is to require a down payment for any customer without a payment track record with you. How they handle the deposit is a great indicator of their overall payment ability. The down payment also reduces your exposure, helps cover costs, and speeds up cash flow. I require a down payment from every new customer and any customer who's doing something different or is starting a very large project.

Make sure your product has value to the customer that is equal to or, preferably, higher than the customer is willing to pay. Poor quality is one of the top reasons for slow pay or nonpayment. We've all fallen victim to the slick salesperson who gets us to buy something we later regret. The customer's approach to "getting even" for poor quality is slow payment or refusal to pay.

Offer an incentive for prepayment. I would rather offer a bonus of some type that increases customers' desire to pay early. When possible, don't deliver without receiving payment. At a bare minimum, review your payment terms with the customer in advance. Doing so, you'll eliminate the excuse that they didn't know when the payment was due.

Keep an eye out for clues regarding changes in the customer's ability to pay between the order date and delivery. I've made that change. Now, clients don't walk out my door with a finished tax return until they've paid or made arrangements to do so. End of discussion; no receivables problems.

Send invoices quicker, especially if you are in a service industry. Don't wait for the end of the month, or even the end of the week. Invoice as soon as the work is completed. When you wait, the value in the customer's mind diminishes dramatically.

After the sale is complete, at every step in the collection process, remember to continually remind the customer of the value received. Don't stop selling. Follow up shortly after the sale to ensure their satisfaction. If you can't call them all, be sure to call the big ones. It also provides a great opportunity to upsell and inform them of complementary products and services.

Create a system that includes a combination of calls and letters that *automatically* go out to past-due accounts. The squeaky wheel, as I mentioned before, does get paid first. So squeak loudly... remaining polite and stressing the value you delivered.

If an invoice goes 60 to 90 days past due, as the owner, you should call. Ensure the customer understands the value your product or service provided and rectify any issues that may have occurred. Ask for payment. If they can't pay, suggest that you'll create a payment schedule to help them as they've been a good customer. Only as a last resort, offer a reduced payment provided it meets the specified deadline.

When all else fails, write off the balance due and forget about it. Don't waste additional time and money suing them. Your time is better spent determining what went wrong in your sales and collection process to avoid a repeat of non-collection in the future. It's also better spent looking for better customers who appreciate the value you provide and will pay for it!

Discounting Is Almost Always Wrong

Almost every business owner, probably yourself included, has been faced with a customer carrying a competitor's ad or even an invoice with a lower price. The immediate reaction is often to match the price. Very simply, price matching is a profit-killing error.

The chart below – "Effect of Discounting on Your Profits" – clearly shows the level your sales must increase simply to achieve the same level of profit without the discounting.

For example, assuming a 40-percent profit margin and with a ten-percent discount, in the chart above we see the result is that you will need a sales increase of 33 percent… just to break even. And this assumes that the 33 percent increase does not also create an increase in operating expenses – a pretty unlikely occurrence.

Effect of Discounting on Your Profits

	If your present profit margin is (%):								
	20	25	30	35	40	45	50	55	60
	To produce same profit, sales increase needed (%):								
Discount Price by:									
2%	11	9	7	6	5	5	4	4	3
4%	25	19	15	13	11	10	9	5	7
6%	43	32	25	21	18	15	14	12	11
8%	67	47	36	30	25	22	19	17	15
10%	100	67	50	40	33	29	25	22	20
12%	150	92	67	52	43	36	32	28	25
14%	233	127	88	67	54	45	39	34	30
16%	400	178	114	84	67	55	47	41	36
18%	900	257	150	106	82	67	56	49	43
20%		400	200	133	100	80	67	57	50
25%			500	250	167	125	100	83	71
30%				600	300	200	150	120	100

A better approach, and from the advice of marketing guru Dan Kennedy, is to see what your competitors are doing and do the opposite: raise prices. Yes, you read that right. The advice is often followed by (and I've said this myself): "I can't do that. I'd lose my shirt." Will you lose customers? Yes, you will. But the real question is: Will losing those customers hurt you? Not necessarily.

In the second chart below you see the amount sales would need to decline after a price increase before your gross profits reduce

> *You're in business to generate profit, not just to generate sales.*

below your current level. As an example, with a 40-percent gross profit margin and with a ten-percent increase in price, you could lose 20 percent of your sales before you'd experience a drop in profit. You could lose one out of every five customer and still break even.

Effect of Raising Prices on Your Profits

	If your present margin is (%):								
	20	25	30	35	40	45	50	55	60
	To produce same profit, sales decrease needed (%):								
Increase Price by:									
2%	9	7	6	5	5	4	4	4	3
4%	17	14	12	10	9	8	7	8	6
6%	23	19	17	15	13	12	11	10	9
8%	29	24	21	19	17	15	14	13	12
10%	33	29	25	22	20	18	17	15	14
12%	38	32	29	26	23	21	19	18	17
14%	41	36	32	29	26	24	22	20	19
16%	44	39	35	31	29	26	24	23	21
18%	47	42	38	34	31	29	26	25	23
20%	50	44	40	36	33	31	29	27	25
25%	56	50	45	42	38	36	33	31	29
30%	60	55	50	46	43	40	38	35	33

Business owners who think that price is the only factor influencing a buyer's purchasing decision will still have trouble swallowing this. They'll also reject the concept of value selling. "That may work for some businesses, but it won't work for me." In my experience, there is no business that cannot demand a premium price on products or services. They do it by marketing in a way that the customer perceives added value over the competitor's lower-priced item. Of course, there's a catch. You must do the hard work of determining what your added value is and communicate it clearly and consistently.

If all of your marketing focuses on price, be very afraid. You'll only have a business until a competitor comes along who's willing to sell the same thing for less. Battling on price is a war you'll never win. The customers you attract will only be loyal until they find a lower price elsewhere. The only way to win is to get out of the battle by focusing on features and benefits that set you apart and deliver more value. Examples of this are different for every business, but better quality and service, longer and comprehensive warranties, money-back guarantees, greater convenience, and 24-hour access are some common ones. You may already offer some or all of these, but... if you don't focus your advertising and marketing on them, your prospects will never know what sets you apart.

Your job as a business owner – and therefore, a marketer – is to **market your products and services with a high perceived value and deliver them with service that wows your customers**. Price only matters when all else is equal. Let your competitors battle in the low-price arena with the likes of Amazon, Walmart, Costco®, and others. It's not where you want to be. Build your business on customers who are willing and able to pay for value.

For example, I don't compete with the big guys – H&R Block®, Liberty Tax®, large CPA firms – and I don't compete with people who want to do it themselves. I want to work with those who are willing to pay for my expertise and advice to save thousands of dollars in tax savings every year. I also offer one-on-one coaching for clients – something the big guys really can't offer.

I have a client who sells medical supplies to the general public. We went to their competitors' sites on the internet and they all said the same thing – high-quality products that you need to take care of loved ones, free delivery, etc. What we didn't see was any mention of the caregivers' problems. So we addressed that since most of the caregivers are making the buying decisions in the first place. We changed the playing field by turning my client into a resource center for caregivers rather than focusing on products for patients. Now prospects who are caregivers see a clear reason to call or visit my client first.

Do This First... Before You Raise Prices

The decision to raise prices is a tough one. I get it; I struggled with it too. How you raise prices can have a big effect on your cash flow and bottom line. Two companies in the same industry that raise prices at the same time can have tremendously different results. Successful price increases depend on timing and the perceived value of your products and services.

First, let's decide if you should raise prices. Are your profit margins where they should be? How do they compare to your industry standard? Have costs increased? Are you charging what you're worth? Do you provide anything of value for which you're not charging? Are you sending the wrong message with your pricing? Too low can be as detrimental as too high; it's perceived as an indicator of low quality or limited expertise.

Second, clarify and actually write down the reasons for the increase, including all the details about the value, benefits, and advantages you provide. This is important. It makes the increase not only palatable but actually appreciated by the customer. If your reason is that costs have gone up, the customer reaction is: "So, what's that got to do with me?" Next write down the disadvantages of a price increase. Refer back to the chart in the prior section. Determine exactly how many customers you can afford to lose.

Third, what can you add to your products or services at little or no cost that boosts value? Increase in prices that include the original product as well as a value-added bonus are much easier to sell. Create tiered offerings: good, better, best. There is a certain percentage who want the best of everything. I've tested this with my own clients. In creating your offerings, remember this: educated customers spend more. We educated them on the good product, and then explained the features and benefits of the better product. Finally, "Here's the best product" with an explanation of why. In our test, most opted for the better category offering. It's basic human nature. Then we added other categories: VIP (higher than best) and Cadillac (highest of all). With this approach, the "best" category is now in the middle – exactly where most people gravitate.

Fourth, determine the amount of the increase. I'm not a fan of one large increase. Step increases? Maybe. Annual increases? Some combination? If you're in the service industry, maybe new customers all get the increased price and existing customers are billed that price with a "customer loyalty" discount then tacked on. Gateway products – those that bring in the majority of your customers – may stay the same with the increase on the add-on products. For me, the gateway product is tax preparation; in medical devices, it may be a walker, a cane, etc.

Fifth, consider the ramifications of both the pros and cons of a price increase. Remember, at a 40-percent profit margin, with a ten-percent increase,

> *Raising fees while focusing on creating added value is the quickest way to increasing your profits.*

you can lose 20 percent of your customers without affecting your gross margin. Honestly, I've never seen it go that high. It's very doubtful that you'd lose one out of every five. The ones you do lose are probably the ones you should lose, giving you more time to invest in retention and gaining new high-margin customers.

Planning the price increase – the when and how – is integral to its success. When should you announce it? How should you announce it? Are there customers who should be told about it in person? People don't like this kind of surprise. That said, you often don't need to actually make an announcement about it. An announcement makes a big deal out of it without a focus on the value added. Have you ever received a price increase letter from your dentist, doctor, or even your hairdresser? It's almost never done. Prices are more elastic than you think, and customers are used to the idea of price increases. Any announcement should focus on the value added, not the price increase. Mention the increase in passing, but the focus of any sort of announcement should be on the benefits you provide. ***The only real reason to announce a price increase is to bring in cash now.***

With one of my clients in the landscaping industry, we changed his price increase announcement in a way that both increased sales and solved his non-busy season cash flow problem. Let's see how.

Here is the first letter he drafted:

Dear Yard Maintenance Customer,

It's been a pleasure to work with you this year. Thanks so much for trusting me to help make your yard one that you can be proud of.

Due to the rising cost of doing business, we will be raising our rates slightly at the beginning of the year. Our rates will increase by $5 for weekly yard maintenance and $10 for monthly maintenance. Our hourly billing rate for all special projects has increased by $5/hour.

As always, we are committed to providing you high-quality yard maintenance and look forward to doing that for you again this year.

Thank you.

You can probably already guess that I rejected this draft. His customers don't care that his costs are increasing. I sent him back to the drawing board, and he returned with this version:

Dear Landscape Maintenance Customer,

It's been a pleasure to work with you this year. Thanks so much for trusting me to help make your yard one that you can be proud of.

As a valued customer, I want you to be among the first to schedule our Special Spring Beautify Your Landscape planning meeting. At this meeting, we will develop a unique plan designed to provide you the landscaping of your dreams. We will also discuss various scheduling needs and any special instructions that you may have.

During this meeting, we will also discuss options to reduce the impact to you caused by the rising costs of material and labor. Our goal is to always provide you with high quality at reasonable prices.

Here's wishing you a wonderful holiday season and a happy New Years.

Better but customers still don't care about your cost increase. However, on the bright side, he introduced a new product that would actually work to boost his cash flow during the winter. We put our heads together and came up with this version:

Dear Landscape Maintenance Customer,

It's been a pleasure to work with you this year. Thanks so much for trusting me to help make your yard one that you can be proud of.

As a valued customer, I want you to be among the first to schedule our Special Spring Beautify Your Landscape planning meeting. At this meeting, we will develop a unique plan designed to provide you the landscaping of your dreams. We will also discuss various scheduling needs and any special instructions that you may have.

I also encourage you to utilize our old fee scale to its maximum. Packages of ten (10) landscape maintenance sessions at the old price are available. They are good for the coming year. Assure yourself great, low-cost landscape maintenance for the next year or give them as gifts to your friends, family, and colleagues to use. They will be thrilled by your thoughtfulness and the professionally groomed yard. Getting the yard work done with no work involved is a gift that no one returns!

Act soon! The appointments and gift certificates at the "old" prices only apply to packages and gift certificates paid for before the end of the year.

Here's wishing you a wonderful holiday season and a happy New Years.

Now, that's a much better letter, and we even snuck in the price increase. Most importantly, we created a way for him to get cash at the end of the year. Plus, he locked in customers – they're prepaid. He generated a referral mechanism as well, and he sold a ton of them!

Yes, you can announce a price increase, but do it creatively and in a way that actually brings in more cash.

Advance Payments Increase Cash

As I just shared in the landscaping letter example, getting payment in advance has multiple benefits. To do so, you must entice your customers to pay in advance (in part or in whole) by offering a discount for doing so.

This program works particularly well for seasonal businesses to negate the usual off-season cash crunch. Besides simply offering advance payment in full, you can also provide benefit to your customers by splitting a large seasonal expense into equal monthly payments – more manageable for them, regular income for you. I actually use this approach myself. It's the secret sauce that combines a discount for customers but keeps a higher profit margin for you in addition to regular cash flow. Here's the checklist to follow:

1. Make a list of products or services that customers purchase at least once or twice a year. It works best for high-ticket items.

2. Design the offer. List the reasons why your customers should jump at this (e.g., upcoming law changes, supply chain increases, anticipated excess demand, etc.). This is one time when I might allude to offsetting cost increases as a reason for a price increase.

3. Determine the "bribe" you'll offer. Again, this is the exception to offering discounts. What you may lose in the discount is made up to you in terms of expedited and steady cash flow.

4. List specific inclusions... and *exclusions*. I learned this the hard way.

5. Make it easy for the customer to pay, and make it easy for you. I strongly suggest only using this if you are setting up automatic credit card charges or ACH payments.

6. Protect your profit margins. While I said I was giving a discount, I was also offering an upsell item. In my case, I added an "audit protection program." The upsell item should be designed to offset the discount. I figured

that if 20 percent opted for the protection program, I'd offset the discount. In reality, 50 percent jumped at it, and I actually made money by having them prepay.

7. Make it a two-year contract without the discount in the second year.
8. Market it to all existing and new customers. Design and draft the copy and test it with a few of your better customers. Follow up in person for feedback.
9. Calculate your profit (and loss) for year one and year two. Ensure that you are covering your costs and are making a nice profit on those customers who elect to prepay!

Certainly, this works best for seasonal businesses – tax prep is certainly seasonal as are landscaping and other outdoor businesses, retail and holiday sales. The goal is to fill in those times when no cash usually flows in. I've implemented this for a number of businesses (including my own), and it's nice to have real cash coming in during typical slow periods.

Inventory Impacts

Inventory is one of your main drains of cash as we touched on earlier. It's amazing how much capital is tied up in inventories for most businesses that sell a product.

Let me share a story to illustrate exactly how this happens. Earlier in my career, I was a comptroller and then CFO for a Coca-Cola® bottling plant in El Paso, Texas. When looking over reports, I saw that another bottling plant in Arizona had two to three times more inventory but only about two-thirds the sales

> *There's cash in them thar inventory shelves. Be sure there's not too much of it!*

volume of our plant. I was sent there to find out why. When I arrived at the plant that evening, the only employee left was the warehouse manager. When I asked why he had so much inventory and how he determined how much to stock, he answered, "The only time I get into trouble is when I run out of product, so I make sure that doesn't happen." Yikes.

There can easily be hundreds of thousands of dollars tied up in inventory in some businesses, and sadly, too many business owners operate on the same principle as that bottling plant – fear of running out. Unfortunately, they set themselves up to run out… of cash. There's huge fear about losing a sale if an item is not in stock, so they stock everything and boast about having the most well-stocked store.

So what is the best way to determine the appropriate inventory levels? Easy: Let your customers tell you. Ask them as they check out: "What is it that we carry that you like best? What don't we carry that you'd like to see on the shelf or what have you wanted that's been backordered?" Don't rely on one person's answer. Keep track and remember: Customers vote with their wallets. The most valuable market research you can ever conduct lies in your sales reports.

Do all the surveys you want, but those answers are only theory. The best data comes from customers putting their money on the table to pay for purchases. You cannot ignore the crucial data you collect every day through customer behavior. Now, with current point-of-sale (POS) software, this data is easy to capture and not very expensive. (If you are not using an automated POS software package, get one now.)

Your floor space and shelf space should be allocated in the same manner that grocery stores do. They allocate space based on what sells. If it doesn't move, they stop carrying it or substantially reduce its inventory level. To do this, your POS should be collecting the following information:

- Sales volume
- Profit margin
- Turnover rate (how often you reorder)

With these three key pieces of information, you will know exactly what your inventory should be. Stop guessing and start analyzing!

Workers Who Are Worth It

You can actually increase your profits by doing staffing reviews. Labor costs are the largest costs for a service business and the second largest for a business that sells products. However, rarely do business owners make any attempt to control it. Maybe they take a stab at it by controlling overtime or insurance costs, but they don't do anything in terms of staffing reviews to ensure they are not overstaffed. Most businesses suffer from "mission creep" – "I need a person for this or that" and someone always seems to need an assistant.

First and at least annually, scrutinize every position and know how it fits into your long-term objectives. Probe all aspects of every job: basic functions, level of work performed, relationship to other roles, etc. Decide if any position can be eliminated or outsourced – either entirely or shifted to another employee. Has anyone been performing tasks that are well outside their assigned responsibility? Ask if all positions require full-time workers or can some be handled by part-timers. Assess if you actually need to hire more to ensure that critical jobs are staffed correctly.

I've been involved in many of these assessments, including during my time at Coca-Cola. Two days of full-day meetings reviewing every single employee and every manager had a long list of why they had to keep every employee. After two long days, we only pared down a janitor and an assistant. The money we spent on the meeting didn't come close to being offset by the salaries of the two people we let go.

In another example, I had a client losing $160,000. When we reviewed labor costs, it had climbed dramatically. We conducted an analysis – without names – and excluded department managers from the meeting. We looked at every position and made the necessary adjustments. Within a year, this company went from a $160,000 loss to a $180,000 gain... with sales being flat.

Labor cost is dramatic. Don't be afraid to make the hard decisions. No one likes to fire people, but at the end of the day, if the business doesn't have the cash flow and profits, everyone loses their job – you included!

Reducing Taxes

In my 30-plus years in business, I've learned that some business owners legally pay fewer taxes than others who make roughly the same amount. I call them my smart business owners, and I want you to be one of them. What do they do differently?

First, smart business owners take tax planning seriously. Why? Tax planning is one of the few guarantees a business owner will ever get. You're guaranteed to pay less in taxes unless you had a loss… and even then, I might be able to get some of your money back. It's a rare thing for me to be unable to come up with some way to save money. I often hear, "I don't have time to worry about tax planning. I hire a good CPA." I am a good CPA and I know that there are very few things we can recommend *after* the tax year is closed that have a real impact on cutting your tax bill. It's just like Cinderella at the ball: The clock strikes midnight, her dress turns back to rags, the carriage is a pumpkin again, and the horses revert to mice.

Tax planning is the same. Once it's January first, all I can do is record history in a way that minimizes your taxes as much as legally possible and doesn't attract IRS attention, but I know there was money left on the table – your money. For me and any CPA, on January first, the number of arrows in my quiver that I can use to dramatically cut your taxes are vastly reduced.

Here are a few examples of the benefits of tax planning rather than "tax recording." A manufacturing company cut their taxes by

> *Smart business owners understand the benefit of tax planning. Be smart.*

$125,000; a retail company by $108,000; a dentist, $22,000; consulting company, $277,000; and a construction company saved over $500,000. Every single thing we did was legal and clearly outlined in the tax law. Like I said, I like my clients but won't share a jail cell with them.

Tax planning works because it gives you time to do things with your business that you can't do after the year closes. It's a matter of being proactive during the year rather than being reactive and dropping off your information with your CPA in the spring.

We start with year-to-date income and estimate sales and expenses for the year, typically in the third quarter to have the most realistic snapshot. Then we create a customized plan that itemizes where tax savings can occur for each line item. Some suggestions may incur out-of-pocket costs, so owners have to determine when and where it is the best use of funds. For example, now may or may not be the right time to save for retirement; cash may be better spent in the business. While I'm a fan of tax planning, I'll also caution you that it's never a good idea to make decisions solely based on potential tax savings.

No one can tell you exactly how much you might save on with tax planning, but it's been my experience that there is always a savings.

Smart business owners also call before making any major financial decisions. They always run their ideas before their tax advisors first. Every CPA has horror stories about money wasted because the business owner didn't think it was important to involve them.

Maybe they got their tax advice from their golf buddy. I had one client who was 59 years and four months old and listened to his buddy who told him he could take money from his IRA at age 59, so he took out $50,000. Too bad he didn't call me – his CPA who'd been doing his taxes for years. Of course, the magic number for withdrawal without penalty is 59 and *a half*. He was about six weeks too early, and it cost him $5,000 in penalties. And that's one of the cheaper stories!

Next, smart owners keep good accounting records. If you don't keep good records, I can pretty much promise you that you are paying too much in taxes. You're not tracking all expenses, not tracking items you purchased from your personal account, not remembering purchases on a credit card… and you have no way to defend yourself if you're audited because you have no documentation to support deductions. Without good records, your tax bill will be higher than you are legally required to pay. Conversely, you may think that the IRS can't really prove how much you made, but that's not really true any longer. They've gotten pretty sophisticated about recreating income, so you'd open yourself up to tax fraud. In my experience, those without good records pay more in taxes than the amount they may think they're "cheating the government out of."

My smart business owners get their records to their tax preparer early. If you plan to show up on April 1st or after with a complicated return, you're actually better off waiting until May or June. You can file for the extension, but keep in mind, you'll still have to pay on time or face financial penalties. You want your preparer to complete your return accurately. Mistakes invariably occur on returns prepared just days before the deadline. And in reality, they're probably not actually mistakes – they were estimates made just to get the return done that turn out to be inaccurate.

Next, smart business owners save for their taxes as they earn the income. If you know you'll be paying $30,000 to $40,000 each year, there is absolutely no reason to wait until tax time to look for the cash. Yes, you're gonna pay the taxes – that's the nature of the beast, so set aside the money as you earn it. Sure, we work hard to cut your tax liability but we can't eliminate it. Make quarterly payments or, if nothing else, sock it away in a savings account so it's there to pay Uncle Sam when it's due. Figure out your tax percentage rate and set that aside from every customer payment that comes in. If through tax planning, we can lower what's due, great. You'll get a refund. Personally, at the end of every week, I look at what I collected and move the 15 percent to a savings account (more than I typically need) and the business lives on the rest.

Finally, smart business owners gain a basic understanding of the tax law. If you've ever gone to a hockey or football game with someone who doesn't know the rules, you know that after the initial excitement, they get bored.

Now, I've played hockey as a kid and follow it with a really good understanding of the rules, but I have no misconceptions that with my knowledge I could be a coach. It's the same with business owners and taxes. I don't want you to think you're an experienced tax return preparer. Even with my decades of experience, thousands of returns prepared in hundreds of industries, I can still be challenged. I work hard to stay up-to-date and do not expect you to be at the same level; however, I do want you to have the basic understanding, so we can work together effectively. You always need to know two things: the information that you want from your tax preparer and the information you need to provide.

Cash Conversion Cycle

The cash conversion cycle is key to get more money into your bank account. Without knowing your business or industry, I know this for sure: Cash is king. Even a profitable business will go out of business without cash. With cash, you can hide a multitude of sins. Very few business owners actively manage their cash. They enjoy creating and selling products and services and feel that cash management is the bookkeeper's job.

Employees expect to get paid, the landlord expects the rent, IRS wants payroll taxes, and oh yeah, you need those lights on? The utilities want their money too.

Again: out of cash = out of business.

Getting more cash is what we've been covering in this chapter. Once a cash flow crisis is averted, for most, it's back to business as usual… until the next crisis.

The best way to solve cash flow problems once and for all is to speed up the complete sales-to-cash process. What is that? The cash conversion cycle starts with marketing to get customers; selling and closing the sale; ordering the raw materials and inventory; getting staff to add value; delivering the product; billing and collecting; paying vendors, staff, and overhead; and repeat.

Whatever cash remains after this process is "cash flow." As business owners, we bring in a lot of cash with our left hands, pay a lot of cash out with our right hands, and hope that there are some leftover pennies in our laps. In a perfect world, what I just described is how it works – collecting on the invoice (the left hand) *before* you have to pay out (the right hand). But you know that we rarely, if ever, live in a perfect world. Typically, payments go out well before cash comes in. And it even gets worse when we factor in those fixed expenses (insurance, rent, utilities, etc.) that have to be paid regardless of when cash comes in. I joke that these fixed expenses are called "overhead" because they constantly hang over your head in your never-ending hunt for cash.

I'll be honest: The reason very few businesses improve their cash conversion cycle is because it is really hard work. You have to look at every step in the process and find ways to improve it. However, the payoff is huge. Amazon is a great example, and they've almost perfected it. Think about the model. Everyone pays with a credit card up-front. Amazon is even willing to keep your card on file to make your next order happen in a single step. Several regional warehouses make it easy for next-day shipping. They've fine-tuned the process to dominate online shopping and even brick-and-mortar stores.

Consider the comparison of two companies. I buy from Company A today, receive it in a week, get the invoice at the end of the month, and pay 45 to 60 days later. Or... I buy from Company B and pay for it today (or at least a deposit), it ships tomorrow and I receive it in a week along with the invoice, and I pay any balance in 45 to 60 days. Company A actually gets my money 90 to 100 days after the initial sale. They have to maintain a large cash reserve to finance my purchase. Company B has designed their sales-to-cash cycle so they receive at least 50 percent before the product goes out the door. They are far less worried about running out of cash.

Don't think that only Amazon can pull this off. I have a manufacturing customer who always struggled with cash... until they changed their policy and now require 50 percent down with every order. Cash problems eliminated. The 50 percent deposit effectively pays for materials and labor. All he ever waits for is the profit.

When I got to Coca-Cola, the typical receivables didn't even flow quickly when checks arrived. The secretary was tasked with opening the mail. Then she forwarded checks the next day to the accountant where they sat there for a day or so when they were then forwarded to the receivables clerk's desk where they might sit... for a week! I quickly made one change – making *copies* of the checks for the bookkeeper and receivables clerk and deposited the cash that day. Doesn't seem like a big deal, but because we got the checks into the bank sooner, the interest income earned actually offset my salary. Small change; huge difference.

> ***Amazon's cash conversion cycle is worth emulating!***

"But that won't work in my industry." Typical pushback comment, and I've made it myself, following CPA industry standards that reflected Company A in the previous example. I made a change, requiring CPA clients to submit to monthly billing via credit card or bank draft. Also, now no one walks out the door with a tax return unless it's paid in full. We explain the policies at the very beginning, so there's clear understanding about payment expectations. I decided to take it a step further. Why can't I get paid in advance? Almost unheard of in my industry. That's when I created the system I explained earlier about offering a discount for monthly payments. All new clients now must leave at least 50 percent down. It also serves to weed out the deadbeats. If they don't want to pay us now, they probably won't pay later either. I also created a number of various service packages that now enable us to enjoy sales and revenue above the industry average.

Here's the crux of what I learned and what I want you to clearly understand: Just because your competitors, heck, even your entire industry, does things one way doesn't mean that you have to follow suit. Don't be afraid to improve how you are being paid! And don't say, "That won't work in my industry" either.

A key to speeding up the cash conversion cycle is eliminating receivables to the greatest extent possible. But... don't overdo it. Some business owners can be so concerned about bad debt that they institute extremely tight restrictions on granting credit. This is okay if your competitors have similar terms. At Coca-Cola, I actually loosened credit terms – but kept a very close eye on payments, reverting any slow payer to COD.

You can also overdo it if you restrict inventory too much. This usually rears up with seasonal products. For products popular for the holidays, customers want them on the holiday, not after, so you probably have to boost inventory accordingly or risk losing the sale.

When it comes to paying vendors, if you overdo it and delay those payments, taken to its extreme, you can risk losing any prompt payment discounts, generating bad credit and higher prices, and become a thorn in your vendor's side. The result is that they won't help you when you need it.

Yes, improve your cash conversion cycle but don't overdo it. Remember: pigs get fat and hogs get slaughtered. Don't be one.

This is an area that is chockful of opportunities to increase cash balances. In Appendix 1, I have included my coaching checklist, "17 Steps to Improving Your Cash Conversion Cycle." Implementing just one idea from this list can potentially eliminate your cash problems and massively increase your profits.

Budgeting Blues

"I hate to budget" you say. Let me reply: "In my opinion, it is a vital tool for running and growing your business."

I don't know anyone who likes to budget. Heck, I'm a CPA and I don't like it. Like you and most business owners, I like to dream of the day when there's enough cash in the bank that I don't have to worry about budgets ever again. But no matter how big any business gets, that's pretty much a fantasy.

So let's stop dreaming and get to work. My budget is broken into three parts:

- Clients and what I expect to collect from them in the next 12 months.
- Categories of work – tax work, consulting, coaching, etc.
- Expenses, both business and personal, identifying the large ones to control costs and save accordingly.

The whole point of budgeting is to ensure you don't run out of cash – obvious! That said, when a budget is set up correctly, it can do so much more. It is a check on receivables: who owes me money and who I need to call for collection. Conversely, since I have monthly programs set up, it works as a double check to ensure that I'm doing the work for each client that I should be doing each month.

A budget also helps you keep an eye on proposals. I use it to track outstanding or pending proposals and what closing the deal would mean to me and the business cash flow. Again, it gives me an incentive to follow up with the prospect.

I can also see the effect of the customer prepay plans on both cash flow and the work flow.

In terms of expenses, you'll want to compare the actual bills to what you've budgeted as they come in. You get a real time snapshot to ensure that you are living within your means. With a budget done properly, you can also know when you'll incur large expenses, allowing you time to control costs and save as needed.

As I mentioned previously, I review expenses twice a year to look for ways to cut them. My budget provides the blueprint for that review. It also provides a look ahead to new opportunities that keeps me motivated to work on those for growth rather than simply putting out daily fires.

These benefits are why I personally spend so much time and energy on an accurate-as-possible budget. I don't know of any business that runs *successfully* without a budget. To design the right type of budget, you probably need to work with a CPA. It will pay off for you and get you past the "I hate to budget" excuse!

Stop Flushing Money Away

There are several ways that bad accounting reduces your profit, and I am always amazed to run into business owners who have no real accounting system – or worse, an accounting system that spits out inaccurate and misleading reports. With software like QuickBooks® that is inexpensive and easy to use, there is simply no excuse for bad accounting. The cost of time and money to set up a good accounting system is easily recovered and always provides a positive Return on Investment (ROI).

Here are the common cash drains caused by business owners who ignore the need for good accounting:

1. Bank overdraft fees caused by not knowing your true cash balance. While online banking has reduced this, and I recommend you check your online balance daily.
2. Unauthorized bank charges – perhaps a bank error, unauthorized vendor billing, unapproved employee purchase. Check your

balance and set up alerts. I receive one every time a charge in excess of $125 goes through.

3. Unnoticed returned customer check. Perhaps you received notice but got busy and forgot about it.

4. Short-term shortages of cash due to inaccurate bank balances. This can lead to interest charges on unplanned but avoidable loans.

5. Not collecting receivables. I know I've been beating this drum, but it is so important to your cash flow! Studies show that the longer you wait to collect a receivable, the higher the chance of never collecting. Your accounting system should reflect timely details about what each customer owes and when it's due – the aging schedule.

6. Lost inventory. Okay, "lost" is a nice way to say stolen. But it can also refer to obsolete inventory that the business owner lost track off. Good accounting identifies it and allows you to attempt to sell at a discount to at least recover part of the cost.

7. Late fees for failing to pay vendors on time.

8. Double payments to vendors. You'd be amazed how often this happens.

9. Paying for merchandise or materials you never receive. If you don't have a good procedure and accounting system set up for purchasing, this can easily happen. Even simple software enables you to create a

purchase order and track it. Before you pay, compare the PO to the packing slip.

10. Failing to notice expense increases. Let's face it, everything goes up in cost. Good accounting lets you compare current pricing against previous. When you notice increases, it may be time to shop around again.

11. Paying more income tax than you need to. Again: if you don't track it, you can't deduct it!

12. Increased employee fraud. A whopping 80 percent of businesses have experienced some form of employee fraud. Good accounting records – frequently reviewed by the owner – reduce this risk and also help catch it sooner when it does occur to reduce the amount of loss.

13. Lost customers. When your review monthly sales data, it's easy to spot customers who are declining or have stopped buying from you. A quick phone call can uncover the underlying reason, giving you time to correct problems on your end before they escalate. On the other hand, when you see new customers, you can call to thank them for their business and open a dialog about everything you can do for them.

14. Missed business opportunities. I started doing QuickBooks training when the product first came out and was too early to market with that offer. Later I realized training

income was increasing dramatically without my doing any marketing. Market research revealed that QuickBooks had now taken hold on the business owners' consciousness, yet they were now looking for help to implement it, so it was time to act and increase our marketing about our QuickBooks training. Without good accounting, we might have missed that trend. Now we've actually seen the trend go the other way due to YouTube videos (including some I've posted), so we've reduced our marketing and only offer training when asked by current clients.

Get your accounting records up-to-date and stop letting cash slip through your fingers!

But I Need Money Now!

"These sound great, Wayne, but I need money now!"

When you're out of money, yes, you need to discover the root cause of the problem, and I understand that takes time – time you don't have right now. We touched on these in the introduction, but it's critical, so let's look again. So where can you find cash?

Knowing where to look is vital. Start by looking inside your business and then working your way out from there. Every option has risks and costs.

First, lower your own compensation or even eliminate your salary.

Second (you probably know what I'm going to say), collect receivables! Review those aging reports and get on the phone. Consider selling invoices, known as "factoring." It costs about four percent of the invoice, but do your due diligence first! Hire a collection agency. Even call customers with outstanding but not overdue invoices and level with them about your situation. Ask for a favor and maybe offer a discount. Create a prepayment plan, as we've covered already.

Lend your business money from personal assets or credit cards. Don't be afraid to use your credit cards in a pinch, but it can be an expensive approach. I've worked with now very successful business owners who'd remortgaged their homes during a cash crisis.

Or, as we covered earlier, family members may offer to pitch in. Ensure this loan is properly documented like any other and pay it back as quickly as possible.

Ask for extensions from vendors. They may be happy to get paid in 60 days rather than not at all.

Again, get a line of credit. ***And again, if you don't currently need cash, now is the time to set this up.*** Banks don't like to lend money to businesses in crisis mode.

Consider bringing in an equity partner and share part of the business in order to get the funding you need. Think long and hard on this one, and get legal and accounting advice to set this up correctly.

There is no painless way to get out of a cash crunch. Go to Appendix 2 to see my checklist: "82 Tricks to Find and Keep Cash in Your Business." It will provide you an in-depth look at how you can solve your cash problems.

Steps to Your 90-Day Profit Reset

- There is a clear relationship between expenses and cash flow. Reduce the former to increase the latter.
- Don't count your chickens…. Until the money is in the bank, it's not doing you any good. You're in business to generate profits, not sales.
- Collecting receivables in timely fashion or, even better, getting paid in advance is the best way to reinvigorate your cash flow.
- Math proves that discounting is almost always the wrong approach.
- Raising prices is never as detrimental as you imagine. Typically, you have to lose 20 percent of your customers before you affect gross margin.
- Your cost increase is never the excuse to raise prices. Your customers don't care about your costs; they care about theirs.
- There's a ton of cash tied up in your inventory. Improve how you control it.
- Take a hard look at labor costs. No one likes to let people go, but failure to do that to improve the business financials might mean everyone loses their job.
- Smart business owners pay only the amount of tax legally required and not one penny more. They understand the value of tax planning.

- Improving your cash conversion cycle is hard work… and worth every effort.
- A good accounting system is worth the investment; otherwise, you might be flushing money away.

Chapter Two:

Re-engage Your Customers

Most business owners overlook the gold mine atop which they sit – their current customers. Notice this chapter isn't titled "Get New Customers." When I begin sales consulting with my clients, the very first thing I have them work on is improving every part of their sales cycle to ***current customers***. The fastest way to grow your business or reset your profits if you're struggling is to market to your current customers.

Amazingly most business owners ignore this… ignoring the gold mine. The first thing they do to increase sales is some form of advertising, either traditional, digital, or both. Outbound marketing has a place, but marketing to your existing customers provides faster impact to your profits. These folks already know, trust, and, hopefully like you.

Before we jump into improving the sales cycle, let's talk about what that is, step-by-step:

1. Convert prospects into paying customers. Count how many prospects you talk to who actually hand over money. It's an important number to know. When I started, this number was about 30 percent. Now my close ratio is closer to 90 percent. In fact, I'm in the enviable position of turning away prospects who are not a good fit.

   Start by measuring your close rate to create a baseline. If you don't know that, you can't measure improvement. Next, identify every first contact point with a prospect and what its goal is (e.g., educate, set up a meeting, sell, etc.). Ultimately, your goal should be to get a customer for life, not a one-time sale. Actually script the first contact in detail. Too often, the first contact occurs with someone in your organization who has not been trained in sales. It makes me cringe when good advertising works to get someone in the door or on the phone who's then greeted poorly or even ignored. That's a huge lost opportunity tied to a lot of lost money.

Keep an eye on your close rate for improvement. If it's not improving, make a single change to your process and measure again. Repeat as needed. If you make more than one change at a time, you won't be certain what actually worked.

2. Now turn your first-time customers into longtime customers. This is too critical to leave to chance. Plan to wow your customers before, during, and after the sale, so they'll never even consider going anywhere else. You and your staff should treat this like a first date, giving undivided attention, determining their true needs, and solving their problems.

Contact your best customers and ask what they like about buying from you and why.

Then contact customers who purchased once but never returned. Find out what you could have done to bring them back.

Give customers an incentive to return often (e.g., frequent buyer discounts, loyalty programs, invitation-only events, etc.), and educate regularly about the value your product or service brings.

> *Repeat after me: An educated customer buys more!*

Stay in contact with your customers to show you care about them. Emails and print newsletters work great to stay top-of-mind with them. They're not walking around thinking about you. You have to remind them.

3. Get them to increase their order size each time they purchase. Plan in advance the related products/services you'll offer during the sales process. McDonald's perfected the art of upselling: "Would you like fries with that?" It's become a running joke, but the joke's on them – it works! Amazon has also honed upselling by showing what other customers also bought in addition to the initial item. How many times have you added to your cart when you saw that?

Train your staff to ask the right questions that lead to add-on sales. Offer it as a solution to a problem they may not even know they have.

4. Get them to refer their friends and others. The best way to get referrals is to do such a good job solving their problems, in a way that's enjoyable and convenient, so that your customers want to flat out brag about you. Wow them. Then simply ask for the referral. But don't just ask for names. People are hesitant to release hungry salespeople on their friends. Instead, ask who may have similar problems. For example, as a photographer, when reviewing wedding photos, ask who else they know may be getting married, graduating, had a baby, or other similar life milestone. You're more likely to trigger their memory and get the referral.

Offer an incentive for the referral. A discount for both them and the new customer helps people overcome their hesitancy about referring. Look at the power of affiliated marketing. I've already cautioned you against discounts, but a discount to get a new customer could well be worth it.

This probably seems like a ton of work. It is. But the rewards are huge. A ten-percent improvement in these four areas can increase sales by 45 percent without the cost of advertising. Consider the amount you spend on advertising to attract new customers, hoping you can increase sales 25 percent. This amount, in reality, is often more than the small business owner can afford. If you concentrate on these four areas, the revenue and profit increase you generate can then allow you to pay for the marketing to bring in brand new prospects for that 25 percent bump. A client of mine did just this and ended up with a sales increase of over 91 percent!

You are sitting on a gold mine, so start digging.

Let's Talk Lifetime Value

This is a critical number to know – the lifetime value of any customer. Every single business owner must know and understand this number. Here's how to calculate it: Take the average price that customers pay for your main product or service and multiply that by the number of years they'll remain a customer. Add to that the average number of referrals they'll send you. Yes, this can get complicated, so work with your accountant if needed to figure this out – it's that important. Check out Appendix 3 for a spreadsheet to calculate the Lifetime Value of a Customer.

Calculating this number often changes the amount you may consider spending to acquire each new customer and how you and your staff treat them. Here's an example: The average personal income tax return customer is charged $250. If I only consider this charge, how much should I spend on my advertising budget and how much time should I spend with each customer? First, I have to know the lifetime value. The average customer stays

> *When you understand lifetime value, you'll stop focusing on single transactions and start building relationships!*

61

seven years and refers two other people. (Hopefully, I'm doing much better!). The lifetime value is $5,250.00. Here's the calculation: $250 x 7 years = $1,750 + ($1,750 x 2 referrals = $3,500) = $5,250.

Now that we know that, let's look at how upselling (getting them to buy an add-on) and cross-selling (getting them to buy something unrelated) can impact the number. Remember: Your current customers are your easiest sales for upselling and cross-selling. Address needs for one product and you'll likely uncover needs for another. It instantly increases revenue and improves your relationship. So let's say I upsell year-end tax planning ($750/year) and one-time QuickBooks training and annual support, totaling $12,450. Obviously much bigger than the original $250 and even substantially higher than the previous lifetime value of $5,250. If I upsell two of their referrals the same way, the lifetime value of that $250 tax return is $37,350!

Now knowing this, how much time and money should I spend to get this client and keep them happy? This is exactly why I spend a great deal of time with new tax return clients, and why we diligently send newsletters, emails, and post Facebook Live videos with tax tips and growth advice.

So… how would knowing the lifetime value of your customers change your perspective? More importantly, how does this number change the amount you'll spend on getting a new customer?

Same Old Excuse

"But that won't work for me" is what I usually hear when I talk to clients about increasing sales to current customers.

"I can't really know who my best customers are because I'm in retail and they come in when they want."

"Raising prices won't work for me because I'm in a competitive area with a highly commoditized product."

The way around both of these excuses is the tiered approach that we covered in the last chapter regarding raising prices. Customers are already used to this. In fact, American Express pioneered this with their gold card offering, and then they added platinum. Finally, there's the elite black card, and who knows what might be coming next. Airlines use tiers in

> *"But that won't work for me" is always an unacceptable excuse.*

the form of economy, business, and first class. Video games offer the "ultimate collector's edition."

Again, start with your basic product, add a better version, and then the best version. Each level has a higher price point plus the customer gets additional perks and added value. Price tiers work because of buying psychology, as I explained before. Some will gravitate toward the best, and a lot of folks will upgrade to the better – revenue you gain over simply having one offer.

Reverse the Risk

You want to dramatically increase sales? Reverse the risk. Lack of trust is what keeps most of your prospects from buying from you. The conversation in their heads goes something like this: "It sounds like it might solve my problem, and I think the price is fair. But what if it doesn't work? What if it fails or breaks? What if I don't get the expected results?" What if....

Get rid of the what if. And that's easy – reverse the risk. You do that by placing the risk on yourself. Before we go further, I'm assuming you are providing a high-quality product or service, and I'm assuming you stand behind your product or service. If you are super confident in your quality, what do you have to be afraid of by placing the risk on your shoulders with a strong guarantee?

Consider the guarantees you've seen and probably received as a consumer. LL Bean has a rock-solid guarantee and return policy: "If you are not 100% satisfied with one of our products purchased directly from *L.L.Bean*, you may *return* it within one year of purchase for a refund." They'll go even further for defects in materials or craftsmanship. I know they stand behind their guarantee because I've used it. I'm certain the sales generated with this guarantee far exceed the cost of the returns/replacements/refunds they issue. And let's not forget about the lifetime value of their customers!

How do you do it? Review your current guarantee. If you tell me you don't have one, I'll ask how you handle the customer who reports to you that your product/service didn't solve their problem. Most answer: "I'd give their money back." So there's your guarantee. You have one; you simply don't use it to your advantage in your marketing.

Now that you understand you have one (even if unwritten and under-marketed), ask if it is bold enough to truly reverse the risk for your prospects and customers. Is it LL Bean rock solid? If not, how can you improve it?

Give your guarantee a unique name that emphasizes the risk reversal. Put it on all of your marketing material and ensure you communicate it to every prospect during the sales process. Don't fixate on the few customers who might abuse your policy. Even if you don't think they have a valid claim, give them their refund, forget about them, and move on. Again, you'll generate far more sales and profit with a strong guarantee than you'll ever give back in refunds.

Where's Your Focus?

Do you want to improve your profit and re-engage customers? Of course you do, so you have to focus on the right ones. The bad news is that most business owners fail to do this. The good news is that it is easy to do because you only have to focus on 20 percent of them. Enter the 80/20 rule.

The 80/20 rule – also known as the Pareto principle – is almost universally true in every business and industry. Very simply, the rule states that 80 percent of the output comes from 20 percent of the input. In other words, 20 percent of your customers generate 80 percent of your profit. Also, 20 percent of your goods and services generate 80 percent of your

> *20% of input always generates 80% of results.*

revenue. Twenty percent of your staff is probably creating 80 percent of the value your customers receive. The scary corollary to this equation is that, as the business owner, eight out of every ten hours you spend in your business does nothing for your bottom line. Ouch. But….

The million-dollar question becomes: Do you know what 20 percent of your efforts are getting the 80 percent of results? Don't worry. I can tell you where to find the answer: your accounting records – your *good* accounting records. You should not just be keeping accounting records so your CPA can generate your tax return. Your record's most important value is to generate daily reports that highlight your best customers, most profitable jobs, and best-selling services and products. Knowing this, you'll know where to focus your efforts to increase profits.

Here's an example: From 2001-2007, I was a school board trustee, including a few years as president. If you are unaware of the role, it amounts to having a non-paying part-time or almost full-time job. This time commitment made it almost impossible for me to seriously market my CPA firm. However, I still managed to double my billings during this tenure. Marketing to new customers would take time I didn't have. I decided to concentrate on selling additional services to my top customers – those who knew, trusted, and liked me, making it easier to sell to them. The Pareto principle at work. In 2007, my top ten customers generated two-thirds of my profit.

Another benefit of focusing on my top customers was that the work they needed done was more interesting. Also, when you concentrate on your best customers' needs, you make it almost impossible for your competitors to steal them. Plus, the likelihood of referral goes way up, and the quality of the referral tends to be high as well. Finally, your very best customers have the ability to pay. (Remember all of our discussion about the importance of timely receivable collection? This is another place it pays off!)

While I no longer serve on the school board (perhaps I've gotten smarter since then), I still concentrate and focus on my best customers. You should do the same thing if you're interested in dramatically increasing both revenue and profits. How?

First, identify your top customers if you don't already know who they are. Who are the top five or ten? Who are in the top 20 percent? Write down what your top five are buying from you. Then determine what they are not buying from you. Contact them and see if they need what else you offer that they aren't buying or don't know about. Share that you understand their pain point and have solved it for others. In my case, I know they don't like paying taxes and I have a proven solution to lower them legally.

During your discussion, explore the other problems they may be facing. Just start the conversation. Take your top five to lunch to see what other solutions you can provide. Then repeat the process with your next five biggest. Then repeat again until you've contacted all the customers that represent your top 20 percent. Once you've gotten through the list, go back and start at the top again – customer needs are always changing.

Why You?

The number one thing you must communicate to your prospects and customers: why they should buy from you. That communication comes in the form of marketing and advertising. Although I'm a CPA, I expanded and hired a marketing specialist and started coaching small business owners about sales and

> *Marketing and sales are vital for one reason – a business without customers is called a hobby.*

marketing. I saw it was an area with which they needed help and there was no one filling that need. Most marketing firms don't even want to talk to you unless you have $10,000 a month to spend on advertising, and some of these folks weren't generating $10,000 a month in revenue.

Few business owners have sales and marketing experience. You might count yourself among them. They're good or even excellent at their craft but being an excellent mechanic, restaurateur, CPA, doctor, attorney is simply not enough. You must be good at your real business, and your real business is not what you think. No matter what you deliver to customers, clients, or patients, *you are really in the marketing business*. You have to get good at attracting customers, enticing them to buy and then buy more and more often, get them to make referrals, and keep them as long as possible. So how do you do it?

Before you start any campaign, you must be able to answer one important question from your customer's perspective: *"Out of all the choices I have, including doing nothing, why should I choose to buy your product or service?"* Very simply: why you?

What is the one major benefit that you offer that your competitors do not offer, cannot offer, or will not offer? This difference is your unique selling proposition (USP). Pushing back with the excuse that your offer is a commodity is lazy thinking and only enhances the customer's perspective that there is no difference.

In order to convert a prospect to customer, there must be a distinguishing factor. Look at your product or service through your customer's eyes. Review every aspect and determine what you can do differently from your competitors in which your prospects and customers will see benefit. Then, create your own category. For me, there are a lot of CPAs, so we created a different category: "Profit Maximizing and Tax Reduction Coach."

Can you specialize in a particular area? Before you're too quick to dismiss that idea, I'll share that there is a bookkeeping firm in El Paso that specializes in truckers. They may not have any greater expertise than other bookkeepers, but by saying they specialize in truckers, they're larger and more profitable than other bookkeepers in the area.

Escape comparison by not allowing competitors to be able to compare your products or services with theirs. Eliminate the possibility of apples-to-apples comparisons. Force them to compare apples to oranges by changing your product in a way competitors can't match. We did

> *Sell what your customer wants and needs but can't get from anyone but you.*

this for our firm by creating a product that combines outsourced bookkeeping, tax preparation, tax planning, and business coaching for a fixed price much higher than what the market is for these services individually. It solves multiple problems for customers and allows me to say, "No other CPA firm in El Paso can give you timely, accurate management reports and business coaching that will help you cut your tax bill and increase your sales and cash balance." Notice how this package quickly eliminates any possible comparisons.

Tell your prospect: No other _____ in this area will solve your _____ by providing _____ for you. Fill in the blanks. When you do, you'll also be answering the critical question of why they should buy from you.

In today's world, unless there is a strong USP, customers buy on one of three things: price, geography, most reviews. Recall an example I shared earlier about a medical supply company. In order to create their USP, they focused on the caregiver rather than the patient and branded as the "caregiver corner," including caregiver blog, website, eBooks for caregivers, and caregiver monthly meetings. This approach was definitely unique and focused on the folks most likely to make medical supply purchases – the caregivers.

Here are three factors in setting up a successful USP, which were introduced in the book *Reality in Advertising* by Rosser Reeves, published in 1961. He argued that being different is simply not enough. To be very successful, your USP must:

1. Offer a benefit that your prospect truly wants, needs, and desires and that they can only get it if they buy your product or service.
2. Deliver a clear difference from competitors' offerings. Your offering should be one that your competitor cannot or does not offer. The difference should be huge.
3. Be strong enough to attract new prospects and customers.

To start, list all of the ways your prospects can satisfy their needs in ways other than buying from you. Next, list all the things you do, including the free ones, that your competitors don't do. From this, look for niches and create your own category. Now, write a sentence for your customer explaining, with all the choices they have including doing it themselves, why they should buy from you. Again, fill in the blanks:

No other _____ in this area will solve your _____ by providing _____ for you.

Referrals the Right Way

Referrals are key to growing your business and attracting more of the types of customers you want; however, most business owners either don't ask for them or ask in a way that makes them look desperate.

If you ask me for the names of others who could use you, I'll balk. You're putting all the responsibility on me. Don't ask, "Do you know someone who can use my service?" Instead, I like to use a method that comes from a position of strength and makes it easy for customer to refer.

One way is to set up a referral prospect file and keep notes on your top customers' contacts. It's easy to do with Google searches or reviewing social media contacts. Ensure your customers don't think you need their help to grow your business. Frame the discussion in such a way that it seems there is limited room for new customers – you're only accepting friends and colleagues of your current customers.

Don't make it seem like you'll become the pushy salesperson, and never forget to thank your customer for the referral – even better, reward them with a small gift or discount.

Referrals are the best source of new business and help you break through the barriers that prospects are now putting up. Increasing referrals is one of the best ways to increase sales. The best way to get them is to always provide outstanding customer service. Add to that a structured referral rewards program. It can be a simple gift certificate, but let's go bigger.

Consider a monthly prize like a big screen TV or iPad for the customer who makes the most referrals each month. Enter their name in a drawing with one chance for each referral. The chance to win a great prize generates more excitement and more referrals. Take it one step further by featuring the winner each month in your newsletter. It creates buzz and incentivizes other customers to refer more. Extravagant? Yes, but small thinking gets small results.

Compare the cost of the prize ($500) to the lifetime value of a new customer. Let's say that's $2,500. If you get 20 referrals a month that you close, that's an additional

$50,000 at $25,000 profit (assuming 50 percent cost). Not a bad trade for a $500 prize. The incentive has to be big enough to get customers to play along. When it is, they'll go out of their way to make the referral rather than dodge the "Who else do you know who could use my services?" question.

Are You Memorable?

My track record with plumbers isn't very good. Those I've used haven't been timely, didn't complete the

> *It's not your customer's job to remember you. It's your job to be memorable.*

work when they said they would, and never came anywhere near the estimate. I needed one around the holidays and got a referral from a friend. Was I ever surprised! He arrived on time, fixed the problem quickly, and didn't charge an arm and a leg. I was so pleased, I referred him to a couple friends and clients. So far so good. Then a few months later and after a rare freeze in El Paso, I had clients who suffered burst pipes and asked if I knew a good plumber. I did… I just couldn't remember his name! And no, despite my daughters' insistence, it's not early Alzheimer's.

My lack of recall is not at all unique. It's exactly what happens to your customers as well. You work hard to please customers and outperform competitors (just like my plumber), but are they remembering you and are you getting the referrals you deserve? Here's the harsh reality: It is not your customers' job to remember you. It's your job to remind them of you, your business, and how you solved their problems.

So what are you doing to earn top-of-mind presence with your customers? What should you be doing?

First, stay in touch. A study published by Bob Thompson, "The Loyalty Connection: Secrets to Customer Retention and Increased Profits" found that 73 percent of customers who stopped buying did so because of customer service. Further digging uncovered that customers felt the business didn't really care about them. The key to creating loyalty is to *regularly remind* your customers that you exist and have the ability to alleviate their pain and address their wants and needs.

Developing loyalty requires a detailed plan for contact. Start by finding out the best way to contact customers, so they're reminded about you and so you stay top-of-mind. Here are 11 ways:

1. Send a monthly newsletter. My business coach, Jim Palmer is known as the "Newsletter Guru," and you should check him out – www.getjimpalmer.com. Get his book, *The Magic of Newsletter Marketing* and study his approach. It's wildly successful. (See the Resource section also.)

2. Send hand-written thank you notes… in an envelope with a regular stamp. It gets noticed because no one else is doing it.

3. Tell them about a new product that will solve their problem. Ask them about problems. Make sure your customers know everything you offer!

4. Thank them for referrals. They've taken a risk, so thank them for trusting you. Rewarded behavior is repeated, so reward them!

5. Remember special occasions – birthdays, anniversaries (include work anniversaries), etc.
6. Share relevant information. "Thought of you when I read this article."
7. Mention that you saw them in the news or that you saw their advertisement.
8. Tell your best customers about a sale or special offer.
9. Have a contest. Everyone loves 'em. Give them an extra chance to win with every purchase.
10. Conduct periodic customer satisfaction surveys. Ask what you're doing right and what could be improved.
11. Write educational blog articles – educated customers buy more. This is where blogging helps. For us, it differentiates us from competitors.

Do what you need to in order to stay top-of-mind. I know I'll wish that plumber did so the next time I need him!

Follow Up, Follow Up, Follow Up

Every business owner should have a plan and a process for following up with every customer after the sale. If that number is too large to make individual follow ups unfeasible, then consider using sampling.

The customer call-back department should be used to follow up with all customers:

- Receive feedback about the service.
- Answer any questions about product use.

- Explore opportunities to sell additional products or services.
- Prompt for referrals (the right way, of course).
- Express gratitude and say thank you.

Employees tasked with making these calls should have good phone personalities and be motivated to provide "legendary" customer service. They should have a script to follow that includes talking points to guide them through various situations. And then, follow up on the follow ups to ensure compliance.

Think you're too small? I had a portrait photographer who massively increased sales without spending a dime on advertising.

A week after a sale, either he or a staff member called each client to ensure they were happy with their order and asked if they needed additional prints. Customers often agreed that they needed more copies.

Then, a month after the sale, he'd call again to thank them and ask if they'd had a chance to frame their portrait. Most had not, which opened the door for him to sell framing… "with a special discount just for you." While many customers passed on framing initially due to the outlay of money for the sitting and portrait, as time passed, they realized they'd need framing to truly enjoy their investment. He'd also correctly asked for referrals.

Six months later, he'd call again with one more pitch: "I'll be destroying the prints you didn't buy soon, so I thought you might want them at a 50-percent discount." This worked amazingly well because customers hated the idea of having prints of their loved ones destroyed. He also offered to frame them using discontinued frames and would once again correctly ask for referrals.

This structured call-back process (handled by the business owner and one staffer) led to a more than 50-percent increase in revenue without any increase to his marketing budget.

With this in mind, now analyze your business and how you can institute a customer call-back process. First, if you need to, go back and reread the section about the right way to ask for referrals. Review your products and services to determine the upsells and add-ons you can offer. Create a calendar for follow ups (one week, one month, etc.) and write your scripts. Be sure to schedule time each week for these calls. Review results and improve as needed. Repeat the calls weekly and watch your revenue and profits increase!

The Beauty of Bundling

To sell more, you don't have to necessarily create new products or services. Instead, create a new "widget" by combining existing ones in different ways to develop a one-stop solution. Cash shortages, of course, happen when bills continue to flow in but revenue doesn't.

Here's a trick I've used successfully to create new monthly income. Every time I finish a tax return for a large customer, I present them an option that includes a combination of the other services I offer that will solve all of their tax and accounting needs. Clients love the idea of using someone they trust and making easy monthly payments. I love it for two reasons. First, I receive monthly payments ranging from $500 to $1,500. It certainly helps to alleviate cash shortages. Second, I increase income by taking a client who paid $1,500 a year for a tax return to paying $5,700 a year for the full complement of services. And some opt for the higher packages, paying quite a bit more annually. They're happy to pay because they are now getting help growing their businesses all yearlong as well as using tax planning to reduce their tax liability. Before, I was simply a necessary evil, helping them complete their return and keep the IRS off their back. Now I'm a trusted advisor who helps them keep more of their hard-earned money.

Bundling is a great way to boost your revenue and explode your profits by solving the majority of your customers' problems. The goal is for you to be a one-stop shop. Look for products and services that naturally complement each other. Before you utter that dreaded phrase, "But it won't work for me," consider some of these examples:

- Car washes selling multi-wash and family packages for a lower price/wash.
- Furniture sales that sell upholstery cleaning products, pillows, and coverings.
- Electronic stores that offer warranties that exceed the manufacturer's.
- Fast food restaurants that offer meal deals.

To create your own new "widget," review all of your offerings that can be combined to solve more than one problem. Next, review your major or flagship offering to determine what you can add to it. Investigate any bundles your competitors may be offering. Set the price point for each bundle, and evaluate the cost of each to ensure your margins are where they need to be. Now, create sales and marketing material for each bundle and plan your campaigns. Don't overlook the importance of training your staff about the bundles and how to sell them.

Here's a bonus tip: If you're selling B2B, offer that annual prepayment discount in December. Many businesses are looking to buy to cut income before year-end. This works especially well with customers who would have been buying from you anyway early in the new year. It benefits them and solves your cash flow problems that often occur in January.

Lost?

You can dramatically increase sales by reactivating latent or lost customers. After selling to current customers and referrals, this is the next easiest sale you can make. Unlike prospects who've never purchased from you, lost customers already know you and at one time trusted and liked you. Most business owners presume customers stop buying because they were unhappy about something. However, sometimes they stop buying because their needs changed. Perhaps they could no longer afford you or they forgot about you.

Often, they've left because a competitor beat your price and now they're unhappy with the poor quality they're receiving. They typically don't return because they're embarrassed and don't want to admit their mistake. Your job, via marketing, is to welcome them back, let them know you've eliminated their reason for leaving (other than price), and introduce new products and services.

A few years back, I worked with a client who had a file room of 6,000 patients that had left in the last 15 years. We created a three-part direct mail campaign that resulted in almost 12 percent response. I assure you – no campaign to cold prospects will generate this type of return.

When selling to past customers, ensure you're communicating the changes you've made to resolve any issues they may have had. Let them

> *After current customers and referrals, latent and lost customers are your next easiest sale.*

know you care about their concerns and will make changes to address them. Use the opportunity to educate them about new products or services about which they're unaware. They may have left because you didn't offer these at the time.

There's gold hiding in latent and lost clients, so at least once a year, go mining for them!

The Two Most Important Words

The two most important words in business are: recurring revenue. Too many business owners start every month at zero. They have to make new sales month in and month out to cover costs. It's really stressful to worry about earning the money to break even. I suspect you know exactly what I'm talking about. I call this the "taxi model": You pick up a fare, deliver them, collect, and look for the next fare.

That's okay when there's plenty of work, but what happens when there's a reduction? What happens during the slow months… other than stress and worry?

I had a client who was building specialized equipment for manufacturing and was making good money, right up until the Great Recession in 2008. Business came to a halt. Equipment orders dried up and bankruptcy loomed. He survived by taking the drastic measures we covered earlier, cutting staff and expenses to the bone and investing personal money. Since then, I've worked with him to develop recurring-revenue products and services that now pay 100 percent of his overhead, so he's enjoying fantastic growth and profits. Today, those special equipment orders that were his meat and potatoes are the gravy instead.

In addition to profits, his peace of mind has increased because at the beginning of each month, he knows he's not at zero. He'll invoice and collect enough to pay all the bills. I've used this as well. Most CPA firms earn their revenue during only six months of the year, so recurring revenue certainly helps during the "off-season."

Let's take a minute to look at the obvious advantages of recurring revenue:

- Even during slow months, money is still coming in.
- Lowers risk during economic slowdowns because you have a cushion to regroup as needed.
- Provides ongoing payments for work already performed.
- Makes it easier to recruit employees due to cash flow certainty.
- Easier budgeting due to stable revenue projections!
- Makes your business more valuable to investors and lenders.

- Let's you spend your time and effort on growing your business rather than starting from zero each month.
- The more recurring revenue you have, the higher the valuation for potential buyers when it's time to sell your business.

Still not convinced? Compare the fate of Blockbuster to Netflix. Both rented movies; however, Netflix was essentially 100 percent recurring revenue while Blockbuster had almost none. What's left of Blockbuster is dismal, while Netflix is easily worth in excess of $220 billion and growing.

There are five levels of recurring revenue:

Level one is a model based on repeat customers. This should be the basic building block for every business – getting customers to return as often as possible. Think grocery and big box stores, dentists, CPAs, etc. They all follow this example. The problem is that nothing stops customers from going to a competitor.

Level two is based on recurring revenue with all of its advantages. Think about insurance agencies that bill every month or quarter. Again, the customer can still make a switch at almost any time.

Level three is recurring revenue that occurs with a contract, like cell phone or cable service. You sign a two-year contract. You can still switch, but now it will cost you to get out of the contract.

Level four is sequential revenue. You generate recurring revenue by continuing to push to upgrade your customers with new offerings. I happen to use Constant Contact® for email. It has a low cost of entry, but the price continues to go up as I add more contacts and need more storage space. DropBox™ is a similar example.

> *"Recurring revenue" must be part of your business vocabulary!*

Level five is repeat revenue with a network effect. The more products and services the customer buys, the more they get out of the experience. At this level, you create a barrier against your competitors and lock in your customers. Think eBay, PayPal, eHarmony, etc.

So what are the best practices to create recurring revenue? Think like your customer and stress the benefit of monthly billing. Here are some rules to follow:

1. Lower pricing. Low-priced items are typically more acceptable to recurring billing, but there are exceptions. Stress the discount built in by paying monthly.

2. Emphasize the benefit. Continually stress the focus of monthly billing and be sure to list at least three benefits that you can spotlight.

3. Use credit cards or ACH debits to make paying you extremely easy. Customers are already accustomed to this. They get a lower price because you aren't sending bills and chasing payments.

4. No contracts. When customers can fire us at any time, it ensures we continue to do our best for them.

"That won't work for me"? Let me tell you, I have not coached one single business for which we could not create a recurring-revenue model – at least one, and in many cases, multiple recurring-revenue streams.

Check out Appendix 4 for "24 Ways to Build Recurring-Revenue Streams." Use this list to brainstorm how you can move your one-time purchase model to a recurring one. Would customers pay an annual fee for the latest version of your product? Is there an educational component for which you could charge a monthly fee? Is there a consumable component?

Look over this list and put on your thinking cap!

#1 Salesperson

If you're looking for your number one salesperson any place other than in the mirror, you're making a mistake. Business owners are their own best salespeople, so they should be out on the floor or in the field selling. You know your business best – it's strengths and limitations. You know exactly how your products or services solve your customers' problems.

On top of this, customers know when they're dealing with someone who knows what they're talking about. It gains trust, and once you have trust, closing the sale is almost guaranteed. You went into business because you have a skill or product of which you are the expert and understand every nuance – all the ins and outs. You know you're better than your competitors.

But now that you've grown your business, you probably find yourself handling hundreds of non-customer-related tasks, so you're off the floor and out of the field, losing your best resource for customer satisfaction.

I've seen it repeatedly with the result being fewer sales and profits. One family business I worked with was a photo store. The father was always, always on the floor making sales and customers knew him. He retired and sold to his son who was always in the back room and rarely on

Your best salesperson? Look in the mirror.

the floor. Did it matter? Actually, this business went out of business very quickly after the son took over. Business owners are the ones who know the customers' needs and how to upsell. It has a huge impact on revenue and then profits. You have to be in front of customers. As the business owner, you are simply the best salesperson.

Ensure that *at least* 20 percent of your time is dedicated to selling and interacting with customers. It doesn't matter if you're an accountant, lawyer, or doctor. There is always selling. Call at least five of your top customers weekly. Discuss their problems and how you can help. Look for sales opportunities and remember that those opportunities are usually disguised as problems in need of solutions.

Yeah, But I Hate to Sell

There's a perfect system for those who hate to sell and it just might be the best system in the new economy. If you say, "I hate to sell," I get it. In fact, for me "hate" might not be the strong enough word. I despise selling, despise cold calling those who perceive me to be an interruption, despise the time it takes to call 100 people just to get 20 appointments, despise the time it takes to meet with the ten prospects who didn't cancel, and despise those who only kept the appointment so I'd leave them alone in the future.

But I also know that every business is really in the sales business. If you don't sell, you don't have customers. A business without customers is a hobby. Plus, those darn employees, landlord, and utility companies all insist on being paid regardless whether you made a sale or not.

Despite how much I despise "selling," I actually close over 80 percent of those who call me with a problem. Since I'm a CPA, prospects came to me, assuming (correctly) that I could solve their tax or business problem.

The problems you solve that your competitors don't or can't is your expertise.

So one day, I simply decided to stop selling. Instead, I waited to be invited by the decision maker to help them solve their problem. I wanted to become the "welcome expert" who was called in to fix their problems.

Here's my "welcome expert" approach: First, I listed my areas of expertise. List what you do better than anyone in your industry. If you don't feel like you're an expert, think of it this way: What's the reason your prospects should buy from you? Sit down now and determine the pain points you alleviate and revisit your USP. In my case, most CPAs only prepare tax returns and financials and help with bookkeeping. I know most business owners want to pay fewer taxes and have more money in the bank, so I decided to be the expert who could help them achieve that.

Next, choose the perfect customer. List every customer or niche for whom you're ideally suited to help. For me, it's small business owners from startup to those with about $5 to $10 million in sales. We adjusted our messaging to then appeal to even tighter niches within that sweet spot – contractors, retail, professionals, food service, etc.

Once you know your perfect customer, list their very specific pain points and what keeps them up at night. What stops them from being successful? If you think about it for only a few minutes, I know you'll come up with a healthy list. I know what small business owners worry about, and I also know that what most CPAs offer doesn't begin to address their pain points.

Next, identify your gateway products or services – those that bring the vast majority of customers to your door. My clients generally show up with tax-related issues, bookkeeping problems, or cash flow and revenue struggles. Have rock-solid solutions to these gateway issues. Figure out how you'll demonstrate and prove that you're the expert to solve these issues. Saying it isn't enough; you have to position yourself properly. Do this by providing free information that indicates you have all the keys to unlocking their needed solution. This information should also agitate their pain, and case studies are a great way to both agitate the pain and demonstrate your ability to solve it.

Technology has truly leveled the playing field, so consider these ways to harness it. Writing is a perfect way to establish your expertise. Regular blogs posted to your site separate you from your competitors and enable prospects to find you. Social media – specifically videos via Facebook Live or something similar – allow you to easily get in front of your customers to talk about solving their problems. Book publishing is no longer "pie in the sky" and truly sets you apart. Speaking in front of an audience whether in person or online (now more prevalent after the pandemic) also establishes credibility and expertise. Consider any trade associations to which you belong and offer to speak at an event. Offer your own webinars. Get local and regional publicity through press release distribution regarding new products, services, accomplishments, staffing, etc.

Outline a process that gets your prospects to welcome you as the expert, and never, ever have to "sell." When you enable prospects to find you and discover what you do, they'll beat a path to your door rather than you having to find them. Think about your own reaction when a salesperson calls. You automatically put up your guard. You don't want to get tricked. Your customers feel the same, so don't get caught selling.

> *In the words of Dan Kennedy, "People hate to be sold, but they love to buy."*

Act like a doctor to find out where it hurts. List all the options that can relieve that pain along with the pros and cons of each. Then itemize what you offer in terms of options, and don't be afraid to rule out those that are not a good fit. It's actually better to disqualify someone who is not a good fit and even recommend them to a competitor so their problem gets solved. Sound crazy? Customers remember this and you've built credibility for the future and for referrals.

Google has changed the way we all do business. Consumers first do research before buying, so that's why what you publish online (blogging, videos, online publications, podcasts, etc.) is so important. It allows you to first be found and then to demonstrate your expertise.

Stop prospecting and being a pest. Instead, position yourself as the welcome expert. Let me share my process for this:

1. Get qualified prospects to request information.
2. Send the information that entices them to contact us for an appointment.
3. Wait for them to contact us, coupled with a series of emails that remind them that they did contact us and always contain valuable information – the stuff contained in your blogs, videos, podcasts, etc. Frequent follow up keeps you top-of-mind for when they're ready to buy.
4. Have them show up, knowing you're the expert who can solve their problem.

Once they're in the door, I use the **PAS** approach: discover the **problem, agitate** that problem that's causing their pain, share the **solution** we provide that has helped many others. I also appeal to emotions because I know people generally make emotionally based decisions and then justify them logically later. The key emotions to tap include: fear, guilt, love, pride, and greed.

Now that I've uncovered the problem, agitated it, and offered a solution, I differentiate myself from my competitors. I know my customers come to me for two reasons to start: paying too much in taxes and/or not making enough money. Here's a recent example: A doctor came in who felt he was paying too much in taxes. So I pulled out our manual of what we do to save on taxes, and I admitted that "There are plenty of CPAs who could help with this. But... very few are doing tax planning. Let me show you the process that enables my clients to save over $5 million in taxes legally in the last four years."

A restaurant and bar owner came in and I uncovered their problem to be a lack of revenue – they simply weren't making enough money. Again, I admitted there were plenty of tax return preparers they could use, but I proved that I was different because I could show them that I focused on helping them to make more money. I do this by sharing our blogs, our Facebook Lives, the eBooks we've published, and my coaching program that helps business owners make more money.

Of course, the next step is to close the sale, but I don't have any tricks because I don't need them. I've established myself as the welcome expert. Prospects typically ask when we can get started. If they don't, I prompt them: "So which solutions do you think will work best for you?"

The focus is always on solving a problem for which I've presented a number of possible options, one of which is hiring us. This only works if you show that you truly care about solving their problem. The second they feel that you're more interested in closing the sale, you've lost them. Follow up and don't get lazy at this point to ensure they haven't changed their mind about hiring you. This first purchase is only the beginning of your relationship. After the sale, be sure you follow up and follow all of the steps I outlined in the earlier section. Don't leave money on the table.

If you find you're having to sell to today's frazzled and overwhelmed consumer, stop selling! Start positioning yourself as the problem-solving expert.

Steps to Your 90-Day Profit Reset

- Never ignore the gold mine that exists in the form of your current customers.
- Focus on four areas – converting prospects to customers, turning first-time customers into long-term customers, increasing order sizes, and getting referrals – and you can substantially increase your revenue without advertising.
- Lifetime value of a customer is a key number. Calculate it!
- Reverse the risk for your clients with a rock-solid guarantee and watch your profits grow.
- Use the Pareto principle and remember that 80 percent of your sales and profits come from just 20 percent of your customers. That's where you should focus.
- Develop your USP and be clear about "why you."
- Referrals are the easiest sales other than your existing customers, and there's a right way and wrong way to go about getting them.

- Stay top-of-mind and be memorable to your customers. It's not their job to remember you. It's your job to remind them.
- Develop a call-back process if you want to more easily increase revenue and profits.
- Create a new "widget" by bundling complementary products and services to keep revenue flowing.
- Re-engage latent and lost customers. After existing customers and referrals, they're your easiest sales.
- "Recurring revenue" are the two most important words to any business.
- You are your #1 salesperson and there is an effective process to follow even if you hate selling.

Chapter Three:

Supercharge Your Profit Margins

While sales and profits are related, they are not directly proportional. Let me say from the start: An increase in sales does not ***automatically*** mean an increase in profits.

A lot of business owners focus on increasing sales, thinking more sales will be the answer to all of their cash flow problems. Did you notice the important word in my statement? More sales should lead to more profit, but it's not a given and it's not automatic. When you increase sales, there are some other increases along with more customers – more vendors and more payables. More customers often lead to more employees. More customers always mean more headaches.

More customers also mean more risk. There are two main times when businesses are prone to filing for bankruptcy: in the first year of existence and right after there's been a dramatic increase in sales. For product-based businesses, it usually occurs around the time they hit the million-dollar mark and staff grows to about ten employees. In service-based businesses, it often happens quicker – a quarter million and five employees.

Why? At these points, it's tougher for the owner to keep a handle on everything going on. If there aren't proper management procedures and accounting systems, it's actually easy to run out of cash. The transition from entrepreneur to manager is one of the hardest to make. It's why fewer than two percent of startups grow to these levels and why so many companies fail to survive.

You can avoid this fate, but it takes work. Are you reading as many business books as possible? Are you looking for a trusted business advisor or coach to guide you through this critical transition? Or are you ignoring this and focusing on selling more, thinking you can grow your way out of any trouble?

The choice is always yours. Do you want to just sell or do you want to have a profit? Profit is what it's always about!

The Bottom Line Is... the Bottom Line

Profits are all that matter. Believing that increasing sales is the most important job for the business owner is a popular myth that causes the vast majority of business owners huge problems. Why? It is focused on exactly the wrong thing. The only thing that counts in business is making a profit. I'm sure you didn't start your business to make a sale just to turn around and send all the money to vendors and employees. Most start and desire to be reasonably prosperous... or even unreasonably prosperous.

Almost without exception, those business owners who suddenly have huge spikes in sales run into cash flow problems. They're so focused on increasing sales that they fail to get the financing and systems in place to support the increased labor costs and inventory when that sales spike does occur. The result is serious financial trouble and even bankruptcy.

> *The only thing that matters? Profit.*

Successful business owners have learned – and some the very hard way – is that the only thing that matters is profit. A profitable business supports the owner and employees while also paying vendors, bank loans, tax liabilities, and investors. Profits provide companies the strength they need to survive the tough times and to take advantage of good business opportunities when they appear.

Successful business owners start every year by creating a profit plan – a sales and marketing plan that focuses on *profitable* sales. Map out a plan that will enable you to hit your profit goal, not your sales goal. When you have a profit plan to follow, you increase your odds of success.

Cash Cows

You know that not all products and services are created equally. On some you can make a ton of money, and on others you barely break even. I'm amazed that some business owners don't know the products on which they make the most money. If they're focusing on low-profit products and ignoring cash cows, trouble is right around the corner and approaching fast. I've actually known business owners who inadvertently price a product below cost and then spend advertising dollars to promote it! Why? Either they're trusting their gut and "back of the cocktail napkin" calculation or they simply don't know their product costs.

So where to start?

Start by calculating your gross profit by product or service. List all your products and apply this calculation to each:

Sales price – (material cost + cost of direct labor [standard rate x standard hours for production] + cost of outsourced work + other direct costs) = gross profit

Have an accountant help set this up because it can be overwhelming. If it sounds like a ton of work, it is. Let me share an example of why it's worth the effort. I had a local Mexican food restaurant opened by two young men who grew up in the business, picking up their fathers' habits. They also believed myths about what was profitable and what wasn't. During a coaching session, I had them go through this exercise, having set up everything on a spreadsheet. They thought I was crazy. "We have 600 items on the menu. You don't mean for us to do this for all of them, do you?" I had them apply the 80/20 rule and do the calculation for the 20 percent of menu items that represented 80 percent of their sales. When they showed up two weeks later, they had done the calculation for... every single item on the menu. When I asked why, they explained that once they got started, they realized that what they **believed** to be their profit on items was not necessarily accurate. The result was that they changed their menu, placing their cash cows in the most prominent places, they stopped offering the low-profit margin dishes on "special," and they added a few dishes that were closer to their higher profit ones. The result of all this hard work? A 25- to 30-percent increase on profits without any advertising. And they paid off a ten-year loan in five years... so even more on the bottom line.

> **Don't trust what you "believe." Use data to get to what's true.**

Let's move on to advanced product cost management, or the ABCs – activity-based costing. When you've calculated your cost and gross profit for your products, congratulations. You're in the top five percent of business owners. Now the bad news: you've just started. It's easy to make costly mistakes if you don't know the total cost incurred throughout the sale – from taking the order to delivering the product to collecting on the invoice.

I had a glass installation customer call me because his sales had increased by 50 percent but his profits had simultaneously dropped by 25 percent! When I did activity-based costing on his major products, I discovered he'd put a new type of glass on sale that was taking his staff three times as long to install. When we adjusted this labor cost, we saw he was losing about ten percent on every sale… at the non-discounted price, and the trouble compounded as he was having a ten-percent off sale. And it got worse. This offer was cannibalizing his cash cow.

To calculate your activity-based cost: *Sales – (sales cost [be sure to include the cost of the time you and your sales staff spend to sell the product] + advertising cost + delivery, set up, freight cost + collection cost) = true gross profits.*

Yes, it's a ton of work, but it is the key to making good profit-based decisions. It allows you to tend and grow your cash cows while limiting or eliminating those products that add little to no profit to your bottom line. Let your competitors focus on the losers. I highly recommend using an accountant to help you calculate your true costs. It always has a positive ROI.

Greasing the Profit Skids

You can increase your profit margin by improving efficiencies. In my 30+ years, having generated thousands of income statements in hundreds of different industries, I know that easily 70 percent or more of the total cost lies in product purchase and/or manufacturing costs and employee costs. However, when it is time to cut costs, few owners look at these areas. Too often business owners complain about bank service charges and phone bills that combined represent less than one percent of the total cost of operations. They'll also spend more time complaining about property tax increases, about which they can do little or nothing, rather than spending time looking for ways to reduce the cost of manufacturing and delivering their products or services.

> *Don't waste time cutting those costs that do not have a large impact on profits. Do the hard work first.*

Why? It's easy. For most expenses, all you have to do is shop for a less expensive provider. The cost to manufacture or provide your products or services is closely tied to the operational processes you have in place. Cutting these costs by changing and improving takes hard work. But as with all the "hard work" I've covered so far, the payoff is huge.

Here are three real-life examples:

In the late '80s, when I was CFO at the bottling plant, my team outlined all the steps in the sale process: from the customer ordering their products to creating and delivering the products, to billing the customer and collecting payment. We then questioned every step in the process with these three questions:

1. Why are we doing it this way?
2. Can we do it more efficiently?
3. Can we do it at a lower cost?

We were constantly told the most dreaded reasons: "That's how we've always done it." Or, "that's how all bottling companies do it." Equally disturbing was that we found different employees doing the same job differently – the result of lacking well-defined processes. A lack of consistency jeopardized quality and is wildly inefficient. Finding a more efficient way was simply a matter of observation. We spent two years documenting every step of every process. The most important results were: dramatic decrease in employee theft, increase in sales and cash flow due to better coordination and communication between sales and production, reduction in inventory due to knowing what to stock and when, and an annual $10 million savings in production cost.

This is not unusual! System improvements almost always result in huge cost savings for every business – large or small.

Remember the Mexican restaurant from my earlier example? Not only did they cut costs, they improved efficiency to the point at which they could seat the customer, take the order, and deliver lunch in about 15 minutes. The lunch crowd could be in and out in about 30 minutes, so they could serve more patrons by turning over tables more quickly, generating more lunch sales than the average restaurant. Plus, the lunch speed has been a fantastic marketing tool for them, bringing in even more customers, especially those pressed for time at lunch.

I've also used system improvements in my CPA firm. Like any service business selling knowledge and time, I'd reached the maximum number of tax returns I could handle. The normal industry approach is to hire more tax preparers. Instead, I took time to develop what I dubbed "the life cycle of a tax return." The changes enabled me to double sales without adding staff. This result only came about because I questioned everything I was doing and why I was doing it – exactly what we'd done at the bottling plant years before. The biggest breakthrough came from looking at what my industry usually did and looking for something different. Most meet with a client when they drop off documents and meet again to review the finished return. It's time intensive and obviously limits the number of returns that can be done. While sitting in a doctor's waiting room, I realized our services were similar – selling knowledge and time. But you only see the doctor for 10 to 15 minutes for only what they can do, and everything else is handled by staff. I modeled this approach. I still meet with every new client to create a plan of action, but everything else changed. I rarely meet with returning clients when they drop off and only review complicated returns. My staff handles everything else. We're doing more returns and our clients are happier. Staff spends more time with them reviewing and answering questions. I still address the unusual and difficult questions and these clients don't feel rushed.

Here are the steps to improve your operational systems:

1. Document all current systems.
2. Create a special action project team whose only job is to improve system efficiency.
3. Question everything:
    *   Why are we doing it this way?
    *   Can we do it more efficiently?
    *   Can we do it at a lower cost?
4. Look at your industry norm and look for a model in a "different but similar" industry (like me in the doctor's office).
5. Calculate your total activity-based costs to ensure you're focusing on cash cows.
6. Eliminate your hiring mistakes... better, hire superstars from now on. Get good at hiring or find someone to help you.
7. Train your employees to use the system.
8. Create a process for continuous review and improvement.
9. Use "hot tickets" to identify and eliminate flaws and holes.
10. Use internal controls to eliminate theft and fraud.
11. Take time management seriously – your time is most important.
12. Learn how to delegate effectively.

At the end of the day, there is no better ROI than improving the efficiency of your business!

But Wait...

"That sounds like too much work and we already have some systems in place." Really? The common complaint I hear from my coaching clients is that they spend all day answering employee's questions and fixing their mistakes. If you're nodding your head, then I'll contend you **do not** have systems in place. If you want to spend your valuable time where it's needed most – focusing on sales and profits – you must eliminate these interruptions.

The best way to do this is to document your systems and processes. Let me suggest that your business has systems in place now... they may simply be undocumented and carried out without an intentional design. Without documented systems, every employee relies on their own system to get the work done. The result? Your customers will likely have a very different experience every time they call, stop in, or interact with your business. Here's the question: Do you want to design the systems for the customer experience that you want or leave it up to your employees?

Besides controlling the customer experience and creating consistent quality, having documented systems makes it easier to manage employees. Training is easy – it's all in the manual. If they forget something, they no longer have to turn to you for the answer. And there are plenty of ways to document besides writing it all out. Capture screen shots (a picture's still worth a thousand words) and create videos of how tasks should be performed. Upload those to a private YouTube

> *Every system can be improved!*

channel and share with staff. Now you're not managing the employee; you're managing the system.

You must believe there's room for improvement (and I assure you there is) so you'll be willing to do the work needed to ***document*** the system. Again, there is already a system in place, even if you didn't design it. Be sure you take control. It's your business. Even if your systems are much more efficient and effective than your competitors, there are always improvements you can make.

So where to start? ***Remember the goal of every business is to deliver a high-quality product or service that meets or exceeds customers wants or desires... and does so profitably.*** If you aren't sure where to start, look for the one area that has the greatest impact on your sales and profits and start there. Every system should be documented, but I get that it's a tall order, so start with the most important ones that can quickly impact your bottom line.

... There's More

Since I just told you that you must document all of your systems, I'll give the outline you need to go about doing so:

1. Write the purpose of each task.
2. Describe what a successful completion of the task looks like.
3. Have the employee outline in detail every step needed to complete the task.
4. Identify the decision points and document them on a decision tree diagram.
5. List all external information the employee needs to complete the task.

6. Review with the employee how this system affects customers, both positively and negatively.
7. Together list ways the system can be improved for greater efficiency, lower cost, and to enhance the customer experience.
8. List the measurement indicators and metrics you can use to determine effectiveness.
9. Design the system to capture the needed data for measuring results and management reports.
10. List the employee's skill needed to perform the task, so you better identify the most logical person for the task. Perhaps a different employee or outsourced entirely.
11. Decide who has the authority to change this system.
12. Decide and document how often the system will be reviewed and by whom for improvement or elimination.
13. Estimate time needed for task completion.

For physical tasks, I highly recommend using video. When video is added to written instructions, it vastly improves the likelihood of accuracy. For computer-based tasks, you can use Zoom or something similar to record screen captures, talking through the process as you are executing it. It really could not be easier.

Keep employees involved to enhance their buy-in and cooperation. Successful system implementation and adherence is the heart and soul of any successful – profitable – business. Documentation is the only way to ensure your business is working the way you envisioned and the way you want.

If you aren't convinced by now about the importance of well-designed and documented systems, and how vital they are to improving your business's bottom line, I have two more books to recommend before you throw up your hands: *The E-Myth Revisited: Why Most Small Businesses Don't Work and What to Do About It* by Michael Gerber and *Work the System: The Simple Mechanics of Making More and Working Less* by Sam Carpenter. If I haven't convinced you, perhaps these authors will!

Just 15 Minutes

You can unlock hidden profits by spending just 15 minutes a week reviewing five reports to massively boost your bottom line.

About the last thing business owners are interested in is spending quality time with their accounting records. I often joke about entrepreneurial ADD. Business owners have so many hats to wear that reviewing the books usually takes a back seat to sales, production, delivery, and collections. The highly successful entrepreneur truly understands that accounting is the language of business and that regular report review is the key to increasing profits, sales, and cash flow.

> *"Nothing is interesting if you aren't interested."*
>
> *~ Helen MacInnes*

Business is not a game of numbers but it is a game of human behavior... particularly yours. Accounting is simply the scorecard to measure behavior and its effects. I call it the

15-minute scorecard, and here are the five essential reports I recommend:

- Weekly profit and loss: Review your income statement weekly to identify what is and isn't working. Where's the best focus for your limited time and resources? Compare results week-to-week, month-to-month, quarter-to-quarter, and year-to-year to identify trends and react quickly. Also compare trends to your industry average.

- Sales reports by products and customers allow you to identify your most profitable products and customers. Know your best customers, focus on them to provide outstanding service and look for opportunities to sell them more. Again, they're your easiest sale.

- Accounts receivables: You already know the most common cause of cash flow problems lies in collection failure. Weekly reviews provide control, prevent surprises, and improve collection probability.

- Accounts payables: Too often, business owners look at the bank balance and think they can make that extravagant purchase. They fail to see they owe vendors more than what's in the bank. Knowing how much cash you need in the next 30 days always improves your chances of meeting obligations. You'll also sleep better at night.

- Cash on hand: Profit can be an opinion, but cash is a fact. Each day, you must know how much you have in the bank, and that knowledge will actually drive you toward a bigger bank account.

Highly profitable businesses are always run by owners who know their numbers. They value the information in their accounting records and often use an experienced CPA to help them analyze them.

Determine what other reports you need to review regularly to cut costs, improve efficiency, and boost sales and profit. Next, design these reports in your accounting program. Then, schedule time for review of these plus the five above and actually schedule it on your calendar. Hire a CPA to help you set these up and tutor you about what to look for in each one. I highly recommend you hire a CPA to review your reports quarterly. They'll often spot trends you won't and their advice always provides a return on your investment.

Special Projects

As you work to improve systems and efficiencies, you'll uncover many projects that need to be completed. Some will naturally fall to a certain employee, but others will not... and those should be assigned to a special action project team.

The purpose of this team is to simply improve the business. It's hard to make improvements amid the chaos of daily operations. Apple does this amazingly well – both in efficiency improvement and bringing new products to market. It is not the result of a spark of genius. It happens by consistently having an organized approach to project implementation.

The keys to the success of your special action project team are:

- Identifying the projects that will have the greatest impact on success – the proverbial low-hanging fruit. This is your job to start, but as teams begin working, they'll point out what needs work next.
- Setting aside time weekly (or at least monthly) for the team to meet and work. Schedule this to underscore the importance of the team's work and your dedication to it.
- Choosing the right team members. Select employees who can offer the most. It's very beneficial to include employees from different departments to broaden the team's perspective.
- Implementing a system to ensure action and completion. Who does what by when! Delegate tasks and be consistent with follow up, so deadlines are met.

During the six years I was CFO at the bottling plant, I used special action project teams extensively, and the result was to increase the profits every year that at least covered the payroll cost of my 30-plus person department. In a single year, we worked on projects that cut production costs by over $10 million annually.

So you're not a big company. Even a single-person company can employ special action project teams. Yes, you'll do the work yourself or hire a profit coach to help. Again, it's always an investment that delivers a positive return.

Back to the Cash Conversion Cycle

We already covered how improving your cash conversion cycle can help your cash flow, and it can also help you boost production capacity.

Be forewarned: There's going to be a lot of math here, so you can also check out the examples at Appendix 5: Case Study of the Affect from Improving the Cash Conversion Cycle. This is a case study from a manufacturing company, and while all manufacturers should sit up and take notice, every business can benefit from this example.

How much you can produce is limited by your buying power, which is the working capital available to you as well as your payables credit limits, which is how much credit your vendors are willing to extend to you. Let's say my working capital is $100,000 and payables credit limit is $200,000, so my total buying power is $300,000. I'm going to make some assumptions here:

Average ticket order price:	$1,000
Total cost of item sold:	-$ 700
Profit:	$ 300

The equation for the total orders possible before a cash shortage hits is:

Buying power / cost of item sold
With that, our example is:

$300,000 / $700 = 429 orders before I run into trouble. How many orders I can process in a year is a function of the number of days between order date and delivery date, which in the example I'm sharing is 23 days. The average number of days between delivery and payment is 60 days. Average days to pay the vendor is 30, and the total from sales to collection is 83 days. Reduce that by the 30 days to pay the vendors and the result is 53 days where cash is tied up.

The total buying power turns in a year – how many times I can repeat the process – is 6.89 times per year (due to complexity, I'm not sharing that actual calculation here). So my total annual capacity is 429 orders per buying power turn x 6.89 turns per year = 2,951. The resulting total sales orders possible are:

2,951 x $1000/order = $2,951,000

Cost as shown above is 70%, so the highest possible profit I can earn is $885,445.

I get that I just threw a lot of numbers at you. But I want to show you how working to improve the cash conversion cycle (marketing, selling, ordering raw materials and inventory, value add by staff, delivery, billing and collecting, paying staff and vendors, and paying overhead) not only improves cash flow but also increases throughput or total orders possible. When you increase throughput, you ultimately increase sales and profit.

Working with my manufacturing customer, we made improvements and cut the delivery date by six days, the average order-to-payment by 15 days, increased the date to pay vendors by eight days, and the total days from sales to collection was cut by 28 days so it was now 25 days. The total of all of these improvements increased the buying turn time from 6.89 turns to 14.75... more than double. This increased the total number of orders possible by 3,369 for a total of 6,320. Same 429 orders now repeated 14.75 times in a year.

So with the same $300,000 in buying power, we could now produce and deliver up to $6.3 million with a gross profit of almost $1.9 million. And this happened without adding people and without adding additional working capital.

	Original Cash Conversion Cycle	Improved Cash Conversion Cycle
Buying Power	$300,000	$300,000
Avg. Ticket Order	$1,000	$1,000
Avg. Total Cost	$700	$700
Total Sales → Collection	53 days	**25 days**
Buying Turns/Year	6.89	14.75
Annual Orders	2,951	6,320
Total Sales	$2,951,000	$6,328,000
Total Potential Profit	$885,445	$1,898,400
Added Profit:		$1,012,955

Looking at the table above based on the case study I just explained, my customer only focused on changing the one highlighted area, and the rest of the math took care of itself, and he put over $1,000,000 extra in his pocket. It is worth your efforts, so work with your CPA to figure this out for yourself.

You Probably Need Help

In this chapter, I've covered only the initial steps that I take with my coaching clients to help them supercharge their profit margins. Let's face it: There are really only two ways to increase your profits when you get right down to it. Either increase prices or decrease costs. Of course, both are far easier said than done.

I've developed a checklist of "55 Ways to Increase Margins." Again, as a business owner, you're in the business of generating profit, not making and selling products or services. Your focus should always be on the profit margin. This check list is available at Appendix 6: 55 Ways to Increase Profit Margins; however, before you stop reading and jump over there, I must caution you. Many of the items on this list can result in serious problems if blindly implemented. Increase prices too much without stressing value and your sales may drop to the point that you may not cover overhead. Decrease costs too much and you risk undermining the quality of your product or service. Either of these errors can drive prospects right to your competitors.

Be sure to put thought into each of the items on this list in developing and executing your plan. I designed this list as a conversation starter and a thought-provoking way to help clients increase their margins. It's highly unlikely that all of these items will be appropriate for your business. However, if even one or two of them helps you successfully raise your margin, it will be well, well worth your time and effort.

Print out the "55 Ways to Increase Margins" and meet with your CPA or profit coach and review each item on the list individually, identifying those that will have the most impact and result in highly increased profits.

Steps to Your 90-Day Profit Reset

- The only thing that really matters is profit. Generating profit is why you're in business.
- Figure out your cash cows and focus on those. It takes work but always pays off.
- Always ask:
    1. Why are we doing it this way?
    2. Can we do it more efficiently?
    3. Can we do it at a lower cost?
- Remember this equation: System improvements = profit increase.
- Even if you haven't designed a system, there is one in place, and it's the one your employees have developed on their own. Don't leave quality, customer satisfaction, and cost containment to chance. Design systems for everything.
- Take 15 minutes every week to review at least these five critical accounting reports:
    1. Weekly profit and loss
    2. Sales
    3. Accounts receivable
    4. Accounts payable
    5. Cash on hand
- Special action project teams can help improve your systems and efficiency… and

they're possible to create and use even in the smallest businesses.

- Sharpening and improving your cash conversion cycle not only helps you improve cash flow, it also enables you to produce more and thus increase profits without access to additional working capital.

Chapter Four:

The Bottom Line

In my more than four decades, I've had the pleasure of working with thousands of small business owners. However, I'd only classify fewer than one percent of these as "highly successful," dominating their markets and industries. That said, every one of these highly successful entrepreneurs has one thing in common: a laser-like focus on taking action.

They understand that success requires consistent improvements and start with a list of long-term business goals. Then they make a list of what has to happen this year to reach those. Next, they break down that list in terms of what has to happen this quarter, this month, this week… today.

Successful business owners know that the secret to massively increasing profits is the combination of good ideas coupled with a laser focus on regular action. Here's the mantra I want you to adopt and follow:

> ### *Good Ideas*
>
> ### *+*
>
> ### *Action*
>
> ### *=*
>
> ### *Massive Profits*

I believe it's so important that I've made this the model for my coaching program.

Think about how much better your business could be if you worked just four hours a week on making the improvements we've covered in this book. Do it for 50 weeks this year, and you'll have worked 200 hours on boosting your profits and improving your business. How many of your competitors are doing that? Or worse: what if one of your competitors does this and you don't?

Successful business owners not only focus on taking action, they also schedule time every month to plan and implement the good ideas that move them toward their goals. I recommend three steps to my coaching clients:

1. Use our "Perfect Monthly Growth Tool" that I'll cover next.
2. Use a monthly process to plan and analyze your marketing and promotion activities.
3. Use weekly delegation meetings to ensure employees are working on those items that move the business toward the profit goals.

Finally, every successful business owner with whom I've worked has hired a business or profit coach to keep them accountable, myself included. They'll help you set a realistic timeline and keep pushing you to achieve what you say you want to do, flesh out your strategic action plans, measure progress, stay focused (it's easy to get distracted by the latest shiny object), and finish one thing first before moving on. They provide encouragement and motivation when you feel like giving up and provide a fresh perspective based on their own broad experiences. And a good coach will challenge you to go where you may be uncomfortable going on your own.

The end result of working with a coach is a massive increase in sales and profits. How? The coach recognizes where you've sabotaged yourself in the past, pushes you beyond those areas, and holds you accountable to do the hard work needed.

The Perfect Monthly Growth Tool

The secret to growing the business of your dreams is consistent monthly improvement. I already suggested you schedule four hours each week to work on your business.

Here's the tool I use (and it can be found at Appendix 7: The Monthly Profit Planning Worksheet, so feel free to print it and follow along). I use it to help my clients quickly concentrate on those areas that will result in the quickest increase in profits.

The form breaks business down to its three basic components: make the money, keep the money, and improve your operating systems.

Making the money: Increasing sales to current customers – once again, in case you've forgotten, these are your easiest sales. Next, increase sales to new customers because you do need to continuously bring in new customers. Finally, improve your sales and marketing systems. You'll write three or four ideas about how you'll accomplish each of these goals in the next month.

Keeping the money: Start with cutting and controlling product costs: cutting/controlling labor costs and operating expenses, and reducing your tax liability.

Improving your operating systems: Yes, this is all a lot of work; however, don't let yourself become overwhelmed. Keep looking for simple, small improvements and make 'em when you find 'em. You are always better served to make incremental improvements and increases than attempting to find and make huge increases. Small increases will continue to multiply over time and allow you to build the business and bank account you've dreamed of.

> *"A journey of a thousand miles begins with a single step."*
>
> *~ Chinese proverb*

2% Growth Model

In a recent interview, the CEO of a company listed in *Entrepreneur* magazine as one of the fastest growing companies was asked about his planning process. His answer was that his goal was to grow by two percent each month. It led to slow, controlled growth that his management team could handle.

My own experience supports this, and I've seen companies incur wild sales increases that result in less profit and even losses. As we covered earlier, when a company has a sales spike, it often lacks staffing, infrastructure, and systems to handle the load. Customer service suffers leading to fewer referrals; quality decreases leading to a lack of repeat customers.

It is difficult, if not impossible, to continue to massively increase sales. But every business can figure out how to make two-percent increases. Make two percent more sales calls; increase your cash conversion rate by two percent; increase advertising by two percent; increase order size by two percent... you get the idea.

Small changes are easier to make than large ones and can be sustained over time. And the really good news is that this approach works like compounding with small increases resulting in a far larger result than you might expect. Two-percent increase per month for two years does not result in a 48-percent increase. It results in a staggering 161-percent increase! (Trust me. I'm a CPA and I did the math.) That two-percent increase in sales and profit will enable your company to double in size every three years.

Stop and ask yourself right now: What can you do two percent better this month?

What's Next?

So... where do you go from here? For starters, you might want to reread the book. I've covered a ton!

And don't forget to check out everything in the Resource section and the Appendix that follow.

There's my private Facebook group (The Profit Maximizer Club) that includes recordings a few times a week about ways to increase your business (https://www.facebook.com/groups/smartprofitmaximizer/)
.

Subscribe to my blog "The Small Business Profit Maximizer":
https://wjb-cpa.typepad.com/wayne_j_belisle_cpa_busin/
and my YouTube channel.

You can also follow me on LinkedIn.

Also, as I already mentioned, hire a coach. In fact, you can hire me. I'll be honest, one of the biggest mistakes I've made in my business was to hesitate to hire a coach. "Heck, I'm a CPA. I know this stuff. Why do I need a coach? I know why businesses succeed and fail." The truth is I could not have been more wrong.

I've actually hired multiple coaches in various niches like marketing or profit building. Sure, I understand profit as much as anyone on the planet, but I was not holding myself accountable. The accountability factor was one of the great benefits of using a coach. As entrepreneurs, we believe we can do it ourselves, but the truth is: we can't. No one can.

We get caught up in the day-to-day activities and often fail to set goals. Plus, we are limited by our own perspectives and experience. A coach will see things that you don't.

So how can I help? First, you can check out my home-study course: 90-Day Profit Reset Coaching at www.theSmartProfitMaximizer.com. Or you can sign up for one of my 90-day live coaching sessions. Join me on Facebook Live or be sure to subscribe to my mailing list to find out when these are going to be offered. You can quickly add yourself to my email list by going to my blog (https://wjb-cpa.typepad.com/wayne_j_belisle_cpa_busin/) and sign up for our email newsletter.

Like I said at the start, there's not too much that's new in business. There have been plenty of recessions that business owners have endured and there have been boom times as well. With a plan and a profit coach, you can always come out stronger, not matter what you face.

So let's make this your most profitable year ever!

Resources:

Facebook Profit-Maximizing Club:
https://www.facebook.com/BusinessProfitMaximizer

Wayne Belisle's Profit Master Academy:
https://www.thesmartprofitmaximizer.com/

Blog: *The Small Business Profit Maximizer!*
https://wjb-cpa.typepad.com/wayne_j_belisle_cpa_busin/

YouTube:
https://www.youtube.com/channel/UCfG-aGyl3Pr9Yws9z5StbsQ

The Referral Engine by John Jantsch

Reality in Advertising by Rosser Reeves

Bob Thompson, "The Loyalty Connection: Secrets to Customer Retention and Increased Profits"
http://hookedoncustomers.com/

Jim Palmer: The Newsletter Guru
www.getjimpalmer.com
The Magic of Newsletter Marketing

The E-Myth Revisited: Why Most Small Businesses Don't Work and What to Do About It by Michael Gerber (Subsequent edition 2004)

Work the System: The Simple Mechanics of Making More and Working Less by Sam Carpenter (Revised 3rd edition, 2019)

APPENDIX

www.ProfitMaximizerPublishing.com/90DayProfitReset

Appendix 1: 17 Steps to Improving Your Cash Conversion Cycle.

Appendix 2: 82 Tricks to Find and Keep Cash Hiding in Your Business.

Appendix 3: Worksheet to calculate the Lifetime Value of a Customer.

Appendix 4: 24 Ways to Build Recurring-Revenue Streams.

Appendix 5: Case study of the Effect on Gross Profit from Improving the Cash Conversion Cycle.

Appendix 6: 55 Ways to Increase Profit Margins

Appendix 7: The Monthly Profit Planning Worksheet

Appendix 1

17 Steps to Improving Your
Cash Conversion Cycle

Why should you concentrate on improving your cash conversion cycle? Improving the sales cycle reduces your investment in receivables, work-in-process, and inventory. This allows you to increase sales without running out of cash.

Many businesses fail when they first start. But another area of danger is when a company is growing faster than their cash conversion cycle works. The company may be profitable but still end up filing bankruptcy because they run out of cash.

Increasing sales is the key to business growth, but improving your cash conversion cycle is the key to surviving when you increase sales.

These are some of the most common steps many successful business owners take to increase their cash balances.

First, speed up your sales cycle to reduce your production costs.

1. Create an automated sales funnel. Most businesses don't have a sales process that:
   1) attracts qualified leads,
   2) converts these leads into customers, and
   3) automatically upsells and cross-sells them additional products and services.

2. Plan the next sale as soon as you deliver the product or service. Your customers are the easiest people to sell to. They already know you, like

you, and trust you. It only makes sense to have a plan to get your next order from them.

3. Look for recurring-revenue opportunities. Almost nothing improves cash flow more quickly than having sales coming in every month. Explore different ways to create recurring revenue.

4. Set up a system for increasing referrals from every customer. People have been burned by giving referrals, so instead I would ask for "quality introductions." Your current customers are the easiest sales. The next easiest are your customers' friends and family.

Next, speed up your product production and delivery.

5. Improve your systems to speed up the production. Systems are the key to quickly delivering a quality product or service every time.

6. Deliver the work quickly. We've had it happen here. I finish some work and then I'm so busy with the next project that I don't notice the first client hasn't come in for a month. Well, if they don't know that the work is done, they're not going to pay the invoice for it! What's worse, a month later it may no longer have any value to them.

Now speed up the collection of your receivables.

7. <u>Send the invoice promptly</u>. This is often overlooked. Obviously, you can't get paid until you invoice. Now if you're in sales, retail, or the restaurant business, this doesn't really apply, since the customer expects to pay at delivery. But if you're in any of the service industries or construction fields, get those invoices out as soon as possible.

8. <u>Consider prepayments with the order</u>. Every business I have worked with that does this never seems to have a cash flow problem. Don't overlook this, even if it isn't normal in your industry.

9. <u>Negotiate progress payments for large sales</u>. Write these into the contract so that your cash received more closely matches what you need to pay your vendors and employees.

10. <u>Collect your receivables</u>. If you can't eliminate receivables using any of the ways we have discussed above, collecting the invoice is the most important thing you need to do. Remember, it's not a sale until the money is in the bank.

11. <u>Offer discounts for prepayment and/or prompt payment</u>. I would only recommend this if you can't get a line of credit from a bank. Interest rates are so low right now that it is often much

cheaper to get a line of credit than offer prompt payment discounts.

12. <u>Sell your invoices</u>. This is called factoring. One warning: Be sure you have good cash management skills and a budget. One problem I see with companies that factor is that they pocket the money that's supposed to be going toward paying their vendors. This causes many businesses to get even further into trouble.

13. <u>Arrange a line of credit with a bank</u>. This is much harder than it used to be. It is more common now to use invoice or job financing.

Finally, control the money being paid out.

14. <u>You can't really put off paying your staff</u>. But you can control employee costs by improving systems so that the work can be done by lower-skilled workers as much as possible. Doing a complete staffing review periodically will eliminate excess staffing. Outsource or use temporary hires for any non-recurring projects.

15. <u>Take more control over when you pay your vendors</u>. Don't be afraid to call your vendors and say, "Hey, I'm getting slow-paying customers right now and I need a little more time. You want it in 15 days. Can I get 30- or 45-day terms?" They have to make a sale, too. Most vendors would rather work with you than risk not getting

paid at all. Try to negotiate longer terms. Don't be afraid to let them know a competitor is willing to give you better terms.

16. <u>Periodically shop for better pricing from all of your vendors</u>. Most business owners stay with who they know. It is easier and usually less risky. Even if you don't want to change vendors, you can use the competitor's lower price to negotiate a better deal from your current vendor.

17. <u>Change your payment date with your landlord</u>. Sure, your landlord wants to get paid on the 1st of the month, but if you can't make it by then, don't be afraid to delay it to the 10th or the 15th of the month. Sometimes you have to call the landlord and say, "Look, the beginning of the month just doesn't work very well for me. Can I pay on the 15th without a late fee?" They're not going to like it, but they're not going to risk losing you, not in this market and especially if you have been a reliable, long-term tenant.

Having cash in the bank is not an accident; it's the result of actively managing all parts of your business, especially your sales-to-cash cycle. So if you want to have more cash in your bank, start with the hard work that we've outlined above.

Appendix 2

82 Tricks to Find & Keep Cash in Your Business

Decreasing Receivables:

1. Speed up your receivables collections.
2. Offer a discount for quick payment.
3. Sell receivables
4. Negotiate collection of past-due receivables by offering discounts for payment.
5. Payment upon delivery – COD
6. Charge interest on late payers. May not collect it. But it provides you leverage when negotiating and will emphasize the importance of on-time payments to your customers.
7. Contract with a collection agency for old receivables. But first, start by having your attorney write a collection letter. This often works better than a collection agency and is usually much cheaper.
8. Institute a receivable line of credit. Many banks are willing to lend up to 80% of the A/R at interest rates that are much cheaper than factoring costs.
9. Accept ACH and credit card payments on any monthly recurring services.
10. "Fire" late paying customers. You are lending them money – it may be time to "call" the loan due and find a better paying customer instead.

Decreasing Inventory:

11. Reduce carrying costs of inventory. Carrying costs include cost of leased space, insurance, taxes, utilities, personnel to manage the inventory, and theft. This can be as high as 10% of the total

inventory cost every year. For older inventory you should:

- o Sell at a discount,
- o Then at cost,
- o Then at a loss,
- o Finally donate it in order to get a tax deduction.

12. Sell large quantities of inventory to bulk discount purchasers.
13. Carry inventory on consignment.
14. Finance your inventory with a line of credit.
15. Just-in-time ordering.
16. Drop shipment of inventory on purchases.
17. Pay the invoice with a credit card and then pay the credit card before the interest accrues. This is a no cost way to increase the amount of time before you have to pay the invoices.

Payables:

18. Negotiate extended terms.
19. Transferring payables to notes payable. Normal is one year at a low interest rate.
20. Take the maximum amount of time allowed to pay your suppliers. Think of these as an interest-free line of credit from your suppliers.
21. Don't buy all in one place. Price check every purchase with multiple sources.
22. Form a buying cooperative with various of your colleagues and buy in bulk with them.
23. Barter products for goods and services.

Bank Loans:

24. Temporary payment reductions to interest only.

25. Negotiate payment delays.
26. If not possible, negotiate interest only payments.

Owners:

27. Reduce distributions to shareholders.
28. Temporarily cut or reduce the owner's salaries.
29. Home equity loans
30. Loans from 401k's
31. Cash in pension plans
32. Funds from investors

Sales/Customers:

33. Have a sale or special promotion.
34. Raise your prices. Make sure they have kept up with rising costs. Many small business owners think they will lose customers. But most expect price increases. Also many times prices are much more elastic than we think.
35. But first, offer to keep the price the same for the next year or two if they prepay now. Be sure to announce it to all current customers, past customers, and your email list.
36. Bill immediately rather than at the end of the month.
37. Customer advance payments.
38. Start requiring customer deposits on all orders. This should be a larger amount for new customers.
39. Collect at the time service. We do that for all tax returns while there is still urgency. Once we file the return, they often no longer seem to "remember" us.
40. Require progress billings on long-term contracts. This is very common in construction contracts.

41. Call your best clients (80/20 rule) and look for opportunities increase sales.

42. Year-end tax deductions prepayments and sales. Many companies need to spend money at the end of the year in order to reduce taxes.

43. On large jobs, plan for "scope creep" and start using change orders when applicable.

44. Improve customer service and control returns.

45. Reduce discounts.

46. Improve sales to current customers by improving lead conversion, upselling, and referrals. Prepare a checklist that has a list of items that the customer could buy based on what they currently are purchasing.

47. Subscription model. If your product is regularly consumed and repurchased several times a year, institute a subscription program in which the customers prepay for the product and delivery.

48. Create a contest to increase referrals. Think big or go home.

49. Create a new "widget" to use as an upsell, cross-sale, or to a new market. An example is a health club that puts together a special package of 12 sessions at a substantial discount.

50. Combine products and offer a discount in order to sell on a monthly retainer. May reduce your gross profit but will help make your cash flow more predictable.

51. Build it for one and then sell it to many. What expertise do you have that can be turned into an

online coaching product? Sell your information and
knowledge you have that improves others' lives.

52. Institute a layaway sales program. These were very
popular prior to the widespread use of credit cards.
53. Invite your past customers back with a special
package for returning.
54. "Fire" your high-maintenance/low-profit margin
customers. Use the extra time (and lower stress level)
to replace them with better quality and higher-margin
customers.
55. Set up affiliate marketing agreements with other
businesses who also sell to your customers. Have
them endorse your products. Payment can be a
percentage of sale, pay per lead, recurring income,
residual income, and two-tier income.
56. Finish your work-in-process, get them billed and
collected.
57. Calculate your gross margin for all your products.
Promote your high gross margin items.

Expenses:
58. To reduce rent—Sublease a portion of the property.
59. To reduce rent—Negotiate discounts or delays from
the landlord. Since the economic turndown, many
landlords are willing since it is better than losing all
of the rent.
60. Change your sales tax reporting from accrual to cash.
61. Renegotiate your insurance and supplier policies.
Make sure you are getting the best deal possible.
Review your policies annually and get at least three
quotes.

62. Change payroll to semi-monthly rather than bi-weekly. Cuts payroll processing costs by lowering payroll from 26 pay periods to 24 pay periods.

63. Only use advertising where the results can be tracked. If you can't track it, how will you know it is working?

64. Do a complete staffing review. Look for jobs that can be outsourced or eliminated entirely.

65. Cut all staff down to four days during non-peak seasons.

66. Don't staff for busy seasons or busy times of the year. Bring in temp or part-time work for those busy times.

67. Hand out payroll checks after 3:00 p.m. on Fridays. Checks won't hit your bank account until Monday.

68. Offer bonuses to employees for cost-cutting ideas.

69. Cancel, eliminate, or discontinue any expense that is not essential to the customer experience.

Income tax management

70. Take year-end tax planning seriously.

71. Payment plan on income taxes rather than paying the tax.

72. Reduce or skip quarterly estimate tax payments.

73. Make sure you have the correct taxable entity. Sub-S corporations commonly often save small businesses between $5,000 to $20,000 per year.

Other assets:

74. Borrow cash value of life insurance.

75. Investment or loans from family and/or close business associates.

Equipment:

76. Dispose of old equipment in order to reduce property tax and liability insurance.
77. Liquidate unused assets using eBay, Craig's list, garage sales, etc.
78. Sell or borrow against real property you own.
79. Sales and leaseback of equipment or real property.
80. Consider leasing equipment instead of buying equipment.
81. Repair rather than replacing equipment.
82. Buy used equipment rather than new equipment.

Appendix 3

Click on this link:
www.ProfitMaximizerPublishing.com/90DayProfitReset

to get the worksheet for service businesses, restaurants, and retail businesses that you can customize to your own business to calculate lifetime value.

Appendix 4

24 Ways to Build Recurring-Revenue Streams

Use this list to brainstorm how you might move your one-time purchase model to a recurring-revenue model. Start by asking the following questions:

- Would customers pay a monthly or annual fee for the latest version of your product?
- Is there an educational component of your product that you could sell a monthly subscription to?
- Are there some consumable parts of your business similar to the way printers need toner and paper and home coffee machines need coffee pods?

Use the following list to brainstorm recurring-revenue ideas for your business:

1. Charge a monthly or annual fee for a monthly download of an educational product related to your business.
2. A monthly retainer to provide a series of services. Examples of this are commonly used by landscapers, pool maintenance companies, house cleaners, HVAC companies, and other service industries.
3. Hosting packages for software products you sell.
4. Sell a repair warranty for any item you sell that you repair.
5. If you don't repair it, find a third-party repair warranty to sell. This is common in the new home market.

6. Tech support for any products or services you may offer. I offer tech support for our QuickBooks coaching products on a monthly retainer basis.

7. Charge a service fee for servicing your products. Too many businesses treat this as a customer support function doing the work for free or well below cost. Instead treat it as a profit center and charge for support.

8. Sell a maintenance contract. Can you copy the copier formula in which the customer rents the machine and pays a maintenance amount per page printed monthly?

9. Can your products be packaged and sold for a monthly fee? Massage therapist could charge a monthly fee for a series of two or more sessions. A chef could charge for home delivery of weekly meals requiring the customer to prepay for four weeks at a time.

10. Membership clubs can be used by any business. A restaurant may sell a monthly membership that offers priority reservations, a 10% discount on all meals, and monthly special members-only dinners.

11. If you sell merchandise, consider a monthly subscription model.

12. Complementary products that would interest your customers that are offered by others. An example of this is a movie theater that makes a deal with a restaurant to sell a special "date night" package.

13. Affiliate products. Check out ClickBank for products that you can sell at a commission that your current

customers would be interested in. Be sure not to overdo this.

14. Write an e-book. Why not you? Many business experts have books that add credibility to their main business and recurring revenue. An e-book can also be used as a lead magnet to your core products.

15. Seminars, audio, and video programs that sell your expertise.

16. Teach others. Create an online course and sell it online. The good thing is the work is done once, and other than occasional updates to the information, this recurring idea will be on auto-pilot.

17. Combine many of your services or a product to create a new "widget" that offers a "complete solution" for your clients. In the book, I provide an example of how I did this in my CPA firm.

18. If you sell a product or service that tends to be used one a year, consider offering a monthly payment plan. Better yet, offer a discount and upsell a complementary product designed to offset the discount. We do this by offering a monthly payment plan for two years of tax preparation and an option to purchase tax audit protection.

19. Licensing of your work systems. If you are above average at some part of your business, consider licensing your system.

20. Training programs on how to use your products or services.

21. Selling your products on a lease-to-own basis. If you're a furniture store or a home medical equipment sales company, add lease-to-own products.

22. Finance your products.
23. Coaching clubs and group coaching programs. Train others in areas of your expertise.
24. Sell a subscription that combines a physical product with a coaching product. We worked with a client that sends a monthly subscription that includes sample marketing supplies with examples of sales material that shows how they can be used by businesses to increase sales.

Appendix 5:

Click on this link:
www.ProfitMaximizerPublishing.com/90DayProfitReset

to get case study of the "Effect on Gross Profit from Improving the Cash Conversion Cycle." This worksheet will allow you to customize it to your own business.

Appendix 6:

EXECUTION PLAN:

55 Ways to Increase Profit Margins

There are really only two ways to increase profit margins. First, you can increase prices. Second, you can decrease the cost to produce and deliver your products or services. Of course, both are easier said than done.

Many of the items listed here can result in serious problems if they are blindly implemented without thought to how they affect the customer and the bottom line.

Increase prices too much and without stressing value, and your sales may drop to where they won't cover your overhead. Reduce costs too much, and your customers will notice that the quality of their product and their service experience has suffered. They will quickly find a competitor who will provide them with what they are used to.

Here is a thought-provoking list of ways to increase margins. While it is unlikely that all of these will be appropriate for your business, if even one of them is successful at raising margins, it will be well worth your time.

55 ways to increase profit margins:

1. Increase your prices.
2. Change your prices often. Customers have been trained to expect rising prices to the point that they seldom notice a one- or two-percent price increase.
3. Review every product's price and change them to a psychologically similar price. Very few customers will refuse to buy from you if your price is $9.97 for a product rather than $9.27. But that 70-cent price increase

represents a 7.55% increase in profits without much of a push back from most customers.

4. When you do offer a discount, choose a dollar price rather than a percentage off. If you sell a $500 item, consider offering $25 off rather than a 10% discount. The $25 is only a 5% discount and research has shown that many customers perceive a higher discount with the $25 discount offer. There is a reason so many people hate math!

5. Review all of your prices for your customers. It is common to have long-term customers who are paying much less than new customers are. Start slowly moving them toward your normal price.

6. Don't compete on price.

7. Reduce direct costs of goods sold.

8. Take all cash discounts from suppliers.

9. Reduce inventory waste and spoilage.

10. Prevent theft.

11. Track all customer returns and damaged goods.

12. Look for "time wasters" from your staff and eliminate them.

13. Install a "live" inventory tracking system.

14. Readjust your sales mix by marketing your most profitable products.

15. Add new products or services with high margins that logically complement your current products.

16. Focus on a new, more profitable niche. I worked with a portrait studio owner who identified high school yearbook pictures as a very profitable niche that led to increased future sales. The high school graduates got

married, graduated from college, and had kids. These are all portrait opportunities.

17. Specialize! Specialists are expected to be more expensive. What can you specialize in that will allow you to charge a premium?

18. Upsell your current customers to higher-priced items.

19. Cross sell. Again, you are looking to drive up the average dollars and margins of every sale. When I do a company's tax return, I use a checklist to see if I can sell them QuickBooks support, business coaching, tax planning, etc.

20. Having a good, better, best strategy when advertising is a must. Draw people in with the low price of a good product and upsell them on the benefits of the better and best products.

21. Train your staff to upsell higher-margin products.

22. Fire your low-margin customers. They drain profits, time, and energy much better spent on increasing sales to customers who see the value you provide.

23. Eliminate, or at least stop promoting, low-margin products where you can't increase the price.

24. Better yet, use these low-margin products to create a widget at a premium price. A widget is a combination of services and products that you offer at a premium price. As an example, we offer business owners a package that takes care of all their accounting and tax needs plus tax planning and business-growth planning. Clients perceive a higher value with this type of product (widget), created by simply combining these products.

25. Stop selling commodities! In my business, tax returns, bookkeeping, and financial statement preparation are

considered commodities customers sees little value in. Worse, they seldom see a difference between me and other providers. Don't sell commodities. Look back at number 24 above for ways to create widgets with a high perceived value that your customers will gladly pay a premium for.

26. Focus on selling products and services uniquely provided by you.

27. Export. A decline in the value of the dollar has created a tremendous opportunity for more profitable sales overseas. In today's world, this is much easier than it ever used to be for business owners of all sizes.

28. Look for ways to reduce delivery costs. A client of mine is switching from delivering one of their major product lines to straight drop shipping from either the manufacturer or a delivery center. The result has been a dramatic decrease in delivery and inventory costs. The increase in margins has had a dramatic effect in their profitability.

29. Know and analyze your gross margins on all your products or services.

30. Track all costs related to the sale and delivery of the product. This should include sales costs, purchasing or producing the product, delivering the product, installing it, warranty work, and collecting the invoice. If you don't measure it, you can't improve it.

31. Create a system to ensure you are getting the best prices for your products.

32. Document the best processes for every step of the sales process. The key is to reduce the time for each job by

simplifying the process and reducing the number of steps required.

33. Implement a process to track all mistakes. Mistakes cost money in time and materials. They will happen, but your goal is to stop making the same mistakes.

34. Get your employees to focus on improving gross margins. They often have ideas that you never thought of.

35. Create KPIs to spot trends, up or down, in your profit margins.

36. For each product, list the features, advantages, and benefits of every major product. Sell the benefits.

37. Reward your sales staff on profit margins, not on sales. Remember, you get what you reward.

38. Talk to your suppliers about different ways to get further cost decreases. Often they will have volume discounts. If you give 80% of your business to one vendor, you can get better service, lower prices, better terms, displays, etc.

39. Check with your vendors to see if they offer co-op advertising dollars.

40. Don't forget to track your consumables. These are usually small items but they can add up.

41. If you are in a service business, provide time budgets for how long you expect a project to take. Without them, employees will often "expand" the job beyond what you negotiated with the client.

42. If you have different pricing levels, make sure your sales staff isn't shifting customers to lower price levels in order to make the sale.

43. Have a system that requires approval of any major discounts.
44. Make sure large orders require a special approval by management. You can survive small pricing errors, but a major error can seriously hurt your profits. This is particularly important for large construction projects.
45. Consider adding service fees. Every business provides service to their customers. Whenever possible, you should consider charging them for these services. You can waive them for your most profitable customers.
46. Don't assume anything. Get out of your office and into the field. As your company grows, you often spend less and less time interacting with customers. This often leads to increases in costs and missed opportunities.
47. Reduce the volume or quantity in your product but maintain the cost. Many businesses have used this strategy. Many chocolate bars are smaller now but still carry the same price.
48. Change the package. I noticed that I can now buy Three Musketeers in the form of bite-size pieces in a bag instead of one bar. A review shows that the price per ounce of candy is substantially higher but the perception is that you are getting more in a more convenient form.
49. Be careful with extended warranties. Many of your sales staff will cover the product even after the warranty period for their best customers to get a sale.
50. Add starter kits to increase margins. The concept here is that when a product is sold, you include all the parts, accessories, and installation, plus a supply of consumable items.

51. Charge a premium for special orders and rush orders. These are services and product sales in which price becomes secondary to a specific need or urgency.

52. Take a non-refundable deposit on special projects and orders.

53. Charge a restocking fee on all returns not caused by your error. Make sure you disclose these fees at the time of the sale to avoid headaches later.

54. Anticipate cost increases. Always communicate with your suppliers so that you will have an early warning of cost increases. Educate your staff and customers on why you are raising prices, so they can redirect their displeasure toward the root cause of the increase.

55. Charge different prices for different distribution sectors. In plumbing supplies, it is common to see one price for consumers and a different price for contractors.

Appendix 7

Monthly Profit Planning Worksheet

Good Ideas + Action = Massive Profits

1) Make the Money:

    a. Increasing Sales to Current Customers:

        i.

        ii.

        iii.

        iv.

    b. Increasing Sales to New Customers:

        i.

        ii.

        iii.

        iv.

    c. Improving Sales & Marketing Systems:

        i.

        ii.

        iii.

        iv.

2) Keep the Money

    a. Cutting/Controlling Product Costs:

        i.

        ii.

        iii.

        iv.

b. Cutting/Controlling Employee Costs:

        i.

        ii.

        iii.

        iv.

c. Cutting/Controlling Expenses:

        i.

        ii.

        iii.

        iv.

d. Reducing Your Income Taxes

        i.

        ii.

        iii.

        iv.

3) Improving Your Operating Systems:

        a.

        b.

        c.

        d.

About the Author

Wayne J. Belisle, CPA has been instrumental in helping individuals and business owners reach their financial goals for more than 40 years. Wayne's focus is helping small business owners grow and prosper with a combination of skilled accounting, tax planning, consulting services, and coaching.

Wayne believes small business is the backbone of what makes America great, and after landing a job at a CPA firm in his sophomore year, he knew he would one day have his own firm. After graduating, Wayne worked in public accounting firms for ten years and than spent six years as the chief financial officer at a regional Coca-Cola® bottling plant, allowing him to experience working with CPA firms from the other side of the equation.

Wayne founded his own CPA firm in 1991, where he is still the owner and CEO. Today, he provides his clients with what they really want and need: a roadmap for profitable growth and the know-how, thanks to his expertise, to pay the lowest taxes legally allowed.

The tax planning side of Wayne's practice, along with an increasing demand for his business coaching, is where he is able to have the biggest impact for his clients. In the last four years, Wayne's tax planning advice has saved his clients over $5 million dollars—all legally!

Wayne's goal of helping business owners massively increase their profits is why he started his award-winning blog, "Small Business Profit Maximizer: Ideas You Can Use to Make This Your Most Profitable Year Ever" over ten years ago.

Wayne also launched a private Facebook group, The Profit-Maximizing Club where he shares relevant videos three to five times each week. In addition, he also created Wayne Belisle's Profit Master Academy where he shares profit-maximizing courses, including two free ones. (You can find the links in the Resource section.)

Even after all these years, Wayne finds immense fun and joy working with business owners to help them build their highly profitable dream businesses!